Unlocking the Word

Unlocking the Word
An Anthology of Found Poetry

Jonas Zdanys
Editor

LITERARY PRESS
LAMAR UNIVERSITY

ISBN: 978-1-942956-53-2
Library of Congress Control Number: 2018945524

Manufactured in the United States of America

Lamar University Literary Press
Beaumont, Texas

For all those who have helped me find poetry
at every turn of every road for so many years

Caminante no hay camino
sino estelas en lar mar.

Recent Poetry from Lamar University Literary Press

Bobby Aldridge, *An Affair of the Stilled Heart*
Michael Baldwin, *Lone Star Heart, Poems of a Life in Texas*
Charles Behlen, *Failing Heaven*
Alan Berecka, *With Our Baggage*
David Bowles, *Flower, Song, Dance: Aztec and Mayan Poetry*
Jerry Bradley, *Crownfeathers and Effigies*
Jerry Bradley and Ulf Kirchdorfer, editors, *The Great American Wise Ass Poetry Anthology*
Matthew Brennan, *One Life*
Paul Christensen, *The Jack of Diamonds is a Hard Card to Play*
Christopher Carmona, Rob Johnson, and Chuck Taylor, editors, *The Beatest State in the Union*
Chip Dameron, *Waiting for an Etcher*
William Virgil Davis, *The Bones Poems*
Jeffrey DeLotto, *Voices Writ in Sand*
Chris Ellery, *Elder Tree*
Mimi Ferebee, *Wildfires and Atmospheric Memories*
Larry Griffin, *Cedar Plums*
Ken Hada, *Margaritas and Redfish*
Michelle Hartman, *Disenchanted and Disgruntled*
Michelle Hartman, *Irony and Irreverence*
Katherine Hoerth, *Goddess Wears Cowboy Boots*
Lynn Hoggard, *Motherland*
Gretchen Johnson, *A Trip Through Downer, Minnesota*
Ulf Kirchdorfer, *Chewing Green Leaves*
Laozi, *Daodejing*, tr. By David Breeden, Steven Schroeder, and Wally Swist
Janet McCann, *The Crone at the Casino*
Erin Murphy, *Ancilla*
Laurence Musgrove, *Local Bird*
Dave Oliphant, *The Pilgrimage, Selected Poems: 1962-2012*
Kornelijus Platelis, *Solitary Architectures*
Carol Coffee Reposa, *Underground Musicians*
Jan Seale, *The Parkinson Poems*
Steven Schroeder, *the moon, not the finger, pointing*
Carol Smallwood, *Water, Earth, Air, Fire, and Picket Fences*
Glen Sorestad, *Hazards of Eden*
W.K. Stratton, *Ranchero Ford/ Dying in Red Dirt Country*
Wally Swist, *Invocation*
Jonas Zdanys (ed.), *Pushing the Envelope, Epistolary Poems*
Jonas Zdanys, *Red Stones*
Jonas Zdanys, *Three White Horses*

For information on these and other LULP books go to
www.Lamar.edu/literarypress

CONTENTS

Introduction

When this anthology of found poetry began to take shape, and as I read many splendid submissions, I realized how interesting and engaging the notion of finding a poem in fact is. We don't usually believe that poems are found like lost objects in hidden corners. We are told, from the time we are first introduced to poetry early on in our school days, that poems are written, typically by special people called poets, usually after that special person is struck by an uncanny inspiration, and then they are crafted, edited, revised, and reordered to make them into those fine objects called poems. And we are told, too, that those things called poems are accessible only after careful study or under tutelage, and only after their deepest meanings are unraveled from their linguistic complications, their thematic complexities.

It is small wonder then that so many people are afraid of poems. Most of us grow up believing that poetry is difficult and that it is best left in the hands of those who have dedicated their lives to its vague mysteries. Because it is therefore often removed from our daily lives—many of us think that we encountered poetry for the final time when we graduated from high school or, at the latest, when we completed that dreaded required semester course in English during our freshman year in college —we don't usually think much about it or much of it. And good riddance, we say, to that impenetrable textbook page.

There is some truth to this supposition. Poetry does have that dimension. It does have some difficult elements and a tangible sense that it is somehow separate from the language of everyday discourse. Perhaps that's so because poems are sometimes, if not typically, created when someone has an experience, whatever it might have been, or imagines something, and seeks to present it through selected language. Sometimes those chosen words can be opaque, and sometimes the language of the poem is hard to understand immediately, because the poet is trying to show us what that full experience is rather than to tell us about it directly. A poem, however else we might consider it, is an aesthetic object, and sometimes poets use images and metaphors and sounds to tell truth indirectly, telling it "slant" in the way Emily Dickinson defines for us, because they believe that the language of every day is not adequate to re-present what they have seen or felt or understood. A poem, in this light, is not a direct communication with a reader because the poet's experience, like all human experience, is something that cannot be conveyed directly. So a poem, even as it shapes and stretches language, sometimes beyond comfortable recognition, in its effort to show or reveal meaning, may have all these difficult elements as part of its essential character.

But there is another dimension of poetry, which this volume in many ways seeks to explore: the commitment to provide accessible lessons about the human community, tell us stories about ourselves, give us perspectives on how our social and cultural frameworks evolve and the purposes they serve, engage us in reflections about how we live, and generate and affirm the necessity and beauty of emotional response. Those are essential human yearnings, indispensable to the fullness of what it means to be human and alive, and poetry, perhaps more than any of the other arts, provides us with a wide-ranging and yet concentrated and foundational awareness of such experiences.

I teach poetry courses, seminars in which we read poetry and workshops in which we write poetry, and during our very first class meetings I tell my students that poems are not just stale pieces of literary art reserved for books. I ask them to consider also the notion that poetry and its lyrical power are everywhere around us, that poetry may be one of the most common forms of art that we see and hear in our lives. That is usually a challenging argument to make because most of us are conditioned to believe otherwise. But I point, in my explanation, in the direction of song and hip-hop lyrics, advertising exhortations, school pageants, church sermons and political orations, and other such similar lyrical exclamations, where there is indeed something needfully poetic about the words and expressions presented. These elements often "sound" like poetry, so the leap to viewing them as essentially poetic is not a great one.

But can there be poetry where none is anticipated or expected? Can we be moved in aesthetic and human response by language that, in effect, stands in counterpoint to the idea of formal written poetry with which we are most familiar? The goal in putting this volume together was to go beyond traditional considerations of poetic texts and beyond those particulars that seem to "sound" like poetry. It was to discover the fundamentals of language itself and to consider if all language might have poetry filtering under and through its surface currents. This anthology came together, therefore, in the commitment to consider how poetry itself might be defined more widely, to affirm that poetry's impulse to tell truth and to show various and essential qualities of human experience are not contained only in texts that are defined traditionally as poems.

The question this collection seeks to address is how might we use words not originally meant to be a poem and turn those words into a poetic frame that comments on these essentials. The underlying and organizing principle of this book is that such words can be discovered, that such found poetry works because the poet who recognizes it is able to find the poetry that exists in ordinary language—even in language that at first seems to struggle against any semblance of the imaginative voice—and to

14

identify or understand the aesthetic possibilities of all words no matter where they originally appear. Found poetry involves an appreciative sense of the innate aesthetic possibilities of all language. And it involves a clear and resonant affirmation that language, by its very definition as an articulation of sound and sense, meaning and mystery, tends to the poetic even if we do not intend it originally to be so.

It may be that not all texts are so inclined. The aspiration, of course, is to use poetic sensibilities to find the right whole text and to ensure its thematic and lyrical/narrative integrity even while possibly restructuring its form in such an affirmation. Our expectation, which I believe has been brought to fruition in these pages, was that the focus should be on the original words in a discovered poetic text, and that the text itself should not be changed, the original language should not be edited or revised, though line breaks, stanzas, and other structural elements could certainly be used, and certainly were, as new frameworks of presentation were shaped.

The sources of found poems in this anthology are remarkably varied, all of them non-literary. They include various kinds of textbooks, scholarly and scientific monographs, popular and self-help books, essays, newspaper and magazine articles, letters, emails, advertisements, speeches, and various other "non-creative" publications. They all reveal the joy of the discovery of the transformative aesthetic elements in everyday language and the poetry that resides not just on some forgotten pages but all around us. And they affirm that poetry is about human beings talking to other human beings, celebrating the joys and complexities of words as vehicles for connection as we exchange them with one another, so that what one has experienced can be experienced by the other, so that we can profess a sense of shared human endeavor and find the access to understanding it that language perhaps best provides.

I am most grateful to Jerry Craven, Director of Lamar University Literary Press, for his suggestion that I put this anthology together. It has been both widely illuminating and great fun to do so. I am grateful as well to Sacred Heart University for granting me time to work on this book and on other volumes. All of those who contributed their found poems to this collection have my deepest appreciation and admiration. I am delighted to be the steward of their remarkable discoveries.

Jonas Zdanys
Sacred Heart University

Vivian Shipley

The Hows and Whys of Invisibility

It is possible to become invisible,
but you must be patient, methodical,
and willing to eat almost anything.
One characteristic spell, recorded
by the British polymath John Aubrey
around 1680, instructs you to begin
by acquiring the severed head
of a man who has committed suicide.
You then bury the head, together with
seven black beans, on a Wednesday
morning before sunrise, and water
the ground for seven days with fine
brandy. On the eighth day, the beans
will sprout, whereupon you must
persuade a little girl to pick and shell
them. Pop one into your mouth,
and you will turn invisible.

If you don't have eight days to wait,
you can, instead, gather water
from a fountain exactly at midnight
(invisibility spells are fetishistic about
time management), bring it to a boil,
and drop in a live black cat. Let it
simmer for twenty-four hours,
fish out whatever remains, throw
the meat over your left shoulder,
then take the bones, and while looking
in the mirror, place them one by one
between the teeth on the left side
of your mouth. You'll know you've
turned invisible when you turn invisible.

—Kathryn Schulz, "Sight Unseen," *The New Yorker*, April 13, 2013.

How to Be Naked in Public

Begin by practicing in private. Sure,
you can be nude in your own shower,
but how about sitting the living room
watching TV? How about having dinner?

The first time you strip down in front
of strangers, do so at a specified nudist
destination—a sauna or a beach where
everyone else will also be unclothed.
To be truly at ease, you have to be naked
for yourself, not for the pleasure of others.

The moments before disrobing are always
the most anxious. On average, it takes
an hour for people to get comfortable
and begin frolicking like 5-year-olds
running around the backyard. Choose
your activities carefully. Swimming is
the easiest for beginners. Volleyball and
other jumping sports are more challenging.
Yoga can be particularly intimidating.

Don't be surprised if you occasionally
experience phantom clothes. Initially,
the parts of your body you are the most
insecure about— genitals, breasts, hips,
moles, whatever—will loom large.
You'll imagine people are looking at
that thing, but they're not. Still, expect
some wandering eyes, including your own.
Looking is normal, but don't stare.

    —Malia Wollan, "How to Be Naked in Public," *The New York Times Magazine*,
August 23, 2015.

How to Teach a Bird to Talk

A single parrot cannot forage for fruit
and watch for predators at the same time;
it depends on its chittering flock
for protection. Therefore, to teach a bird
that can talk—parrots, parakeets or mynas,
for example—to talk, find one that
for lack of better options thinks of you
as its flock. Don't get an old disappointed
bird. Buy a baby bird. Specifically opt
for one bred in captivity (or rescued)
rather than one snatched from the wild,
spending as much time as possible
the first several months talking
to your bird in gentle tones, reassuring
it as you would a young child. Don't
hurry them to talk. They need to feel
security in the heart first. Once the bird
has confidence in you as a companion
and reliable food source, start repeating
simple phrases. First you say,
You are very good.
How are you my dear?
I love you.
Many trainers reward learning with nuts
or seeds; though they occasionally
treat the bids to a sip of milky chai tea.
As a bird starts showing aptitude,
ratchet up the difficulty and repetition
by recording your voice and playing
it back to the bird for up to three hours
a day. A person will be bored by this.
But a bird will never bore.

      —Malia Wollan, "How to Teach a Bird to Talk," *The New York Times Magazine*,
March 15, 2015.

When Is Silence A Lie

What does a question mark do?
It looks and acts sort of like an ear,
waiting at the end of a sentence
for an answer. So what is the effect
of a question without a question mark?

Consider, for instance, the jarringly
flat statement, "Where are you going."
The voice, ominously, fails to rise.
Curiosity has been replaced by something
else: terror, accusation, exhaustion.
It's the kind of thing you might hear
at 2 a.m. in a dark room as you try
to sneak out the front door. No answer
is expected. No answer will satisfy.

Do extreme circumstances mitigate lies.
Why was Louis Till, the father of Emmett Till,
court-martialed and hanged in Italy
by the United State Army in 1945? Did he
really commit the crimes he was accused of?
What else might have happened? How deep
do the layers of American injustice run?

Why would anyone reading the tale
today challenge its impartiality.
Will a moment finally emerge in which
a collection of lies offers access to truth.
Some questions have no answers.
Why pretend otherwise?

—Sam Anderson, "When is silence a lie," *The New York Times Magazine*, April 30, 2017.

Does the Balloon Crew Have a Balloon Crew?

We contain whole ecosystems
of resistance to ourselves.
I, for instance, have something
strange that happens when
I stand in a high place. It's like
a hot-air-balloon crew in my feet
When I look over the railing
of the Golden Gate Bridge,
the crew pulls its little flame cord,
and I can feel the basket starting
to rise, a terrifying lifting
sensation at the bottom
of my shoes, and I have to step
quickly away from the edge
and walk off to someplace low.
Such alienation could go on forever.

—Sam Anderson, "New Sentences," *The New York Times Magazine,* October 22, 2017.

Larry D. Thomas

If Campus Carry

(of guns)
had been in
effect when
I was in

Miss Steele's
first grade at Grim
Elementary, I
would have never

made it to the second
grade. Reflecting
back to the days
when I was a college

journalism professor,
carrying a gun
would have been
too much of

a temptation for me,
but I've since
mellowed. Modern
education should not

involve gunplay,
and wisdom
was never
gained with a gun.

—George A. Covington, "Education, guns, and wisdom," *Big Bend Sentinel*,
September 14th, 2017.

Maria Mazziotti Gillan

Requiem for a Four-Year-Old

Mark Warner was four years old
when he died in a Paterson slum. These days
even the people in his old neighborhood
can't remember his name.
"All I know is a little boy died here. Nobody don't talk about it."
The words are spoken casually by a tall, slender woman
with orange-red nail polish. She gives her name
only as "Tee." No last name. On this block
of Broadway in Paterson, where used crack vials
are scattered at the curb and winos
hang out all day outside a liquor store,
people don't give their full names,
Tee is nineteen. She lives in apartment 6,
the same apartment where Mark Warner lived and died.
Standing on the rickety front stoop under a broken window,
Tee says: "Everybody here now wasn't here then."

"Sometimes I just give him a couple of slaps,"
Michael Thomas, Mark's stepfather says.
"But this time I hit him a while."
In the color pictures of Mark Warner,
Mark's lower lip is split
and large purple bruises distort most of his face and body.
Four round scars, old cigarette burns, mark his buttocks.
The coroner believes the welts on his back
are from a whipping with a belt or a wire loop.
Assistant Passaic County Prosecutor,
Marilyn Zdobinski, shakes her head in disgust.
"These are the crimes
that people do not think happen," Zdobinski says.
"But people beat kids every day.
Last week, Mark's twenty-one-year-old mother,
Alvira Warner Thomas, stood silently
in an empty Passaic County Courtroom;

She was sentenced to four years probation
and ordered to seek counseling. Michael Thomas was sentenced
to ten years
without parole. "He is very depressed,"
his lawyer says.

—*The Herald News*, Paterson, NJ, February 13, 1988.

Jayden

Jayden de Leon, age 7, lived on Rosa Parks Boulevard
with his mother and his sisters.
Jayden was shot through a window following a commotion
outside his house, a three-story multi-family across the street
from a liquor store and a car repair shop.

Everyone in the apartment, Jayden's grandmother
and great-grandmother, his sisters, his cousin
was hysterical, but Jayden asked for the phone,
called 911, said "I've been shot" and gave his address.

The police and ambulance arrived within minutes.
Jayden remained calm throughout.
His mother said, "I know the streets are dangerous,
too many drugs, but I can't afford to move."

For many, the street where Jayden lives
offers cheap, stopgap housing.

"It is a place to leave," neighbors said.

Empty lots line both sides of their house.
Patches of grass with empty bottles
of Remy Martin and Budweiser.
Cars rumble by blasting loud music.

Two blocks to the north is School 10.
One block north is Church of God of Prophecy.
"If you want to live here, you've got to be a survivor,"
a 15-year-old neighbor, Frederick David said,
"it's straight surviving."

    —*The Herald News*, Wednesday, March 2, 2016.

Noxious Smog Descends on Tehran

This week a yellow blanket of smog
has settled in for what is typically a winter-long stay.
Reza Shajiee, the prominent hipster,
posts a picture of himself on Instagram
wearing a mask under his motorcycle helmet.
The text reads, "My city is better than yours,
its air is better than yours."
He posts an emoticon wearing a gas mask.
"No one can solve this,"
he said, "and it's getting worse."
Schools were closed for a second day.
Many citizens stayed home
as the capital was covered
in a particularly noxious cloud
for the fifth day in a row.

Every fall, pollution gets trapped
by the Alborz Mountains
that hug the city.
It happens often.
It's hardly news anymore.

For most Iranians,
the problem is so huge,
so complex,
it is better to pretend
it isn't there.

The government announced that 412 people
had died from the pollution in recent days.
Officials admit the pollution causes the premature death
of about 45,000 people each year.
The hipster said "I'll move out at the first opportunity."
But he kept driving around on his chocolate-colored Vespa
churning out smoke.
"What else to do?" he said.

—*The New York Times*, November 15, 2016.

A. C. Jerroll

Condemned to Be Rich

There be many men that are by others taken
to be serious and grave men, whom
we contemn and pity. Men that are taken
to be grave, because nature hath made them
of a sour complexion;
          money-getting men,
men that spend all their time,
          first in getting,
          and next, in anxious
          care to keep it;
men that are condemned to be rich, and then
always busy or discontented: for these
poor rich-men, we Anglers pity them
perfectly, and stand in no need to borrow
their thoughts to think ourselves so happy.
No, no, Sir, we enjoy a contentedness above
the reach of such dispositions, and as
the learned and ingenuous Montaigne
says, like himself, freely,
          "When my Cat
and I entertain each other with mutual apish
tricks, as playing with a garter, who knows
but that I make my Cat more sport
than she makes me? Shall I conclude her
to be simple, that has her time to begin or refuse,
to play as freely as I myself have? Nay,
who knows but that it is a defect
of my not understanding her language, for doubtless
Cats talk and reason with one another,
that we agree no better: and who knows
but that she pities me for being no wiser
than to play with her, and laughs and censures my folly,
for making sport for her, when we two play together?"

—Izaak Walton, *The Compleat Angler*, 1653.

To Own Me for Her Master

The air is most properly mine, I and my Hawks
use that most, and it yields us most recreation.
It stops not the high soaring of my noble, generous
Falcon; in it she ascends to such a height
as the dull eyes of beasts
and fish are not able to reach to; their bodies
are too gross for such high elevations;
in the Air my troops of Hawks soar up on high,
and when they are lost in the sight of men,
then they attend upon and converse with the Gods;
therefore I think my Eagle is so justly styled Jove's
servant in ordinary: and that very Falcon,
that I am now going to see, deserves no meaner a
title, for she usually in her flight endangers
herself, like the son of Daedalus, to have her wings scorched
by the sun's heat, she flies so near it,
but her mettle makes her careless of danger;
for she then heeds nothing, but makes her nimble
pinions cut the fluid air, and so
makes her highway over the steepest mountains
and deepest rivers, and in her glorious career looks
with contempt upon those high steeples
and magnificent palaces which we adore
and wonder at; from which height, I can make
her to descend by a word from my mouth, which she
both knows and obeys, to accept of meat from my hand,
to own me for her Master, to go home
with me, and be willing the next day
to afford me the like recreation.

—Izaak Walton, *The Compleat Angler*, 1653.

Pour Upon Your Carp

Take a Carp, alive if possible;
scour him, and rub him clean
with water and salt,
but scale him not:
then open him; and put him,
with his blood and his liver,
which you must save
when you open him,
into a small pot or kettle:
then take
      sweet marjoram,
      thyme, and parsley,
of each half a handful;
      a sprig of rosemary,
      and another of savoury;
bind them into two or three
small bundles,
and put them in your Carp,
with four or five
whole onions,
      twenty pickled oysters,
      and three anchovies.
Then pour upon your Carp
as much claret wine
as will only cover him;
and season your claret well
      with salt,
      cloves, and mace,
      and the rinds of oranges
      and lemons.
That done, cover your pot
and set it on a quick fire
till it be sufficiently boiled.
Then take out the Carp;
and lay it, with the broth,
into the dish; and pour upon it
      a quarter of a pound of the best
      fresh butter, melted,

and beaten with half a dozen
spoonfuls of the broth, the yolks
of two or three eggs,
and some of the herbs shred:
garnish your dish with lemons,
    and so serve it up.

—Izaak Walton, *The Compleat Angler*, 1653.

All Parts Fit for Generation

It is agreed by most men,
that the Eel is a most dainty fish:
the Romans have esteemed her
the Helena of their feasts;
and some the queen of palate-pleasure.
But most men differ about
their breeding: some say they
breed by generation,
as other fish do; and others,
that they breed, as some worms do,
of mud; as rats and mice,
and many other living
creatures, are bred in Egypt,
by the sun's heat
when it shines upon the
overflowing of the river Nilus;
or out of the putrefaction of the earth,
and divers other ways.
Those that deny them to breed
by generation, as other fish do,
ask, If any man ever saw
an Eel to have a spawn or melt?
And they are answered,
That they may be as certain
of their breeding as
if they had seen spawn;
for they say, that they are certain that Eels
have all parts fit for generation,
like other fish, but so small
as not to be easily discerned,
by reason of their fatness;
but that discerned they may be;
and that the He and the She Eel
may be distinguished by
their fins. And Rondeletius says,
he has seen Eels cling
together like dew-worms.

—Izaak Walton, *The Compleat Angler*, 1653.

A Bastard Breed

Some say, that Breams and Roaches
will mix their eggs and melt together;
and so there is in many places
a bastard breed of Breams,
that never come to be either large or good,
but very numerous.

—Izaak Walton, *The Compleat Angler*, 1653.

Wally Swist

Love, Not a Commandment, but Spontaneous Soul Movement of the Inner Self

Where there is disharmony, there is no love.
The circle closes. Where there is no love,
There can be no fulfillment. Yet, love
Cannot be commanded, nor can it be
A commandment. The more it is tried,
Due to conscience and obedience, the less
Does it succeed. Where love exists,
There must be all fulfillment. Where lack
Of fulfillment exists in a life, it is a sure sign
That somewhere, the soul has not yet learned
To love. The simple equation is often
Overlooked, the words may be understood.
When love exists, there must be physical health,
Which is one of the great desirable factors
In human life. Love is a purifying force.
When love is lacking, to that degree, all sorts
Of negative emotions cause ill health
When the trouble remains sufficiently
Long unrecognized. When love exists,
There must be successful human relationships
Because there is no fear, no distrust, no illusion.
For love can flower only on the substantial
Soil of reality and fearlessness. Where one
Perceives the truth, one does not trust
Or distrust in the wrong place. One accepts
The other as he is and adjusts one's own
Feelings to this reality. There is no necessity
For groping in the dark, fearfully half distrusting,
Being thrown between one's needs and one's fears.
Love and self-confidence are inevitably
Interdependent. Where love is lacking, the psyche
Must be confused. It works both ways—
It is equally true to state that where confusion exists

Love must be lacking. When love exists, all conflict
Must be eliminated. Loving seems such a risk,
So dangerous, so threatening, so irrevocable.
Nothing could be farther from the truth.

—"Love, Not a Commandment, but Spontaneous Soul Movement of the Inner Self," Pathwork Guide Lecture 133. In *Velocity,* Chicago: Virtual Artists Collective, 2013.

Act of Consecration

Lord Jesus Christ, I offer you this prayer as a vessel
to You, the Lord. I sanctify myself.

I consecrate myself today anew, without reserve to
Your Heart. I consecrate to You my body,

with all its senses, my soul with all its faculties, my
entire being—absolute.

I consecrate to You all my thoughts,
words, and deeds; all my sufferings and labors, all

my hopes and sorrows, consolations and joys.
In particular, I consecrate to You this poor heart of

mine, so that it may love only You, so it may be
consumed in its devotion in the fire of your love.

I place my trust in You without reserve, and hope for
the remission of my sins through your infinite mercy.

I place within your hands all my cares,
my every anxiety. I promise to love You and to honor

You until the final moment of my life; and to spread
devotion to Your Sacred Heart.

Do with me what you will, Jesus.
I deserve no other reward except Your greater glory,

Your holy love. Take this offering of myself, and give
me a place within Your divine Heart forever. Amen.

—Father Ralph DiOrio, "An Act of Consecration," a healing prayer service.

Patricia J. Goodrich

Transportation Security Administration
Notice of Baggage Inspection

To protect you
and your fellow passengers,
the Transportation Security Administration
(TSA) is required by law
to inspect all checked baggage.

As part of this process,
some checked bags are opened
and physically inspected.
Your bag was among those
selected for physical inspection.

During the inspection,
your bag and its contents may have been
searched for prohibited items.
At the completion of the inspection,
the contents were returned to your bag.

If the TSA security officer was unable
to open your bag for inspection
because it was locked,
the officer may have been forced
to break the locks on your bag.

TSA sincerely regrets having to do this,
however TSA is not liable for damage
to your locks resulting from this
necessary security precaution.

    —TSA-OSO Form 1000 (Rev. 1-13-2010) found in luggage on almost all flights
national and international since 2001.

Silver Liner Sheath

Designed to wear under any liner
without compromising suspension!

Antimicrobial—
eliminates odor causing bacteria and fungus

Anti-odor—
inhibits bacteria growth, neutralizes ammonia proteins

All natural—
100% safe and non-toxic silver, no chemicals

Thermodynamic—
cooler in summer, warmer in winter

Therapeutic—
high conductive performance for more comfort

Anti-Static—
has very high electrical conductivity

Silver Liner Sheath
with the unique advantage
of X-static Silver

The perfect solution
for amputees

—Comfort Products, Inc., Croydon, Pa. 19021. Package insert for a liner sheath.

Vicki Collins

Mountain Tunes

Sing down the moon,
Abraham's daughter,
for down in the valley,
we'll gather at the river
on an unclouded day.
A man of constant sorrow
never dies nor slumbers,
but weeping sad and lonely,
my darling, declares, "O Death,"
for he is weary and needs rest.
At the church in the wildwood,
we will bury Barbara Allen's
little rosewood casket,
covered with a rose of Sharon,
beneath the willow in the pines.
Fair and tender ladies will meet
down by the river to pray,
and over in Gloryland,
an angel band will play
that old time religion,
so the circle won't be broken
by the scarlet tide.

—Old Appalachian gospel and bluegrass hymns.

The Good Wife's Guide

· Have dinner ready. Plan ahead, even the night before, to have a delicious meal ready on time for his return. This is a way of letting him know that you have been thinking about him and are concerned about his needs.

· Most men are hungry when they come home and the prospect of a good meal (especially his favorite dish) is part of the warm welcome needed.

· Prepare yourself. Take 15 minutes to rest so you'll be refreshed when he arrives. Touch up your makeup, put a ribbon in your hair and be fresh looking. He has just been with a lot of work-weary people.

· Be a little gay and a little more interesting for him. His boring day may need a lift and one of your duties is to provide it.

· Clear away the clutter. Make one last trip through the main part of the house just before your husband arrives. Gather up schoolbooks, toys, paper, etc. and then run a dust cloth over the tables.

· Over the cooler months of the year you should prepare and light a fire for him to unwind by. Your husband will feel he has reached a haven of rest and order, and it will give you a lift too. After all, catering for his comfort will provide you with immense personal satisfaction.

· Prepare the children. Take a few minutes to wash the children's hands and faces (if they are small), comb their hair and, if necessary, change their clothes.

· Children are little treasures and he would like to see them playing the part. Minimize all noise. At the time of his arrival, eliminate all noise of the washer, dryer, or vacuum. Try to encourage the children to be quiet.

· Be happy to see him.

· Greet him with a warm smile and show sincerity in your desire to please him.

· Listen to him. You may have a dozen important things to tell him, but the moment of his arrival is not the time. Let him talk first—remember, his topics of conversation are more important than yours.

· Make the evening his. Never complain if he comes home late or goes out to dinner, or other places of entertainment without you. Instead, try to understand his world of strain and pressure and his very real need to be at home and relax.

· Your goal: Try to make sure your home is a place of peace, order, and tranquility where your husband can renew himself in body and spirit.

· Don't greet him with complaints and problems.

· Don't complain if he's late home for dinner or even if he stays out all night. Count this as minor compared to what he might have gone through that day.

· Make him comfortable. Have him lean back in a comfortable chair or have him lie down in the bedroom. Have a cool or warm drink ready for him.

· Arrange his pillow and offer to take his shoes. Speak in a low, soothing and pleasant voice.

· Don't ask him questions about his actions or question his judgment of integrity. Remember, he is the master of the house and as such will always exercise his will with fairness and truthfulness. You have no right to question him.

· A good wife always knows her place!

—*Housekeeping Monthly*, May 13, 1955.

J. C. Todd

THICC

So there I was describing to my Intro to Creative Writing
    students
the importance of The Battle of Hastings in 1066
and the different valences of Anglo Saxon and French words
in the context of words that they now found dangerous,
    evocative, meaningful
when they taught me the word "thicck." O, OED
let's add this one! I am so old. I cannot keep up.

    Urban Dictionary: THICCK: a girl with big boobs and
butt

The double "c" is brilliant, I think.

        Ahem... "Thicc"   even   better!

The origin of "thicc" comes from certain patterns of spelling
    within the Cripps.
 The letters "CK" are often used by their rival gang, the
    Bloods,
to abbreviate "Cripp killer". Thus, the spelling of words
    that include c+k
are often changed to a double cc, as to remove the self-
    disparaging acronym.

    We can see this in "Succ" and "fucc".   (Excuse
the
      vulgarity).

The Battle of Hastings, man.

    The battle of Rosecrans today.

41

So, not a French root. But is it Germanic or
Anglo-Saxon

when it comes to word choice? Must be
rooted in German:
"dick" meaning fat or thick.

Well, would you Adam and Eve it! All this
rabbit
(and pork) about street language, Michael
and
not a
dicky (bird) about Cockney Rhyming
Slang. It
makes me feel a proper Uncle Dick.

—A Facebook conversation initiated by Michael Martone on September 19, 2017,
with responses from Amy Margolis, Loyd Van Tuyle and Miles Gibson.

Chivas Sandage

Invisible

I never saw them
with my own eyes.
And I never
heard of them. I never thought
of them. In my fifty years,
I have never seen
a gay man. I see flies,
I see mosquitoes,
but I have never
seen a gay man.

—Heda Saratova, member of the Chechen Human Rights Council.

Van Hartmann

Found Poem

Chief of Staff
cannot say he wasn't warned
lunch a memorable breakfast
gathered around a long table,
intellectually and temperamentally
unfit
hard truths
thinking,
God bless him.
Godspeed. Good luck
he doesn't have a prayer.

—Chris Whipple, "Who Needs a Controversy Over the Inauguration?" Reince Priebus Opens Up About His Six Months of Magical Thinking, *Vanity Fair*, March 2018.

Crossword Diplomacy

Sci-fi Iran
and Iraq
primitive dangerous
luxury hotel Rex
mythical lion
White House Stop!
playing in the dark
like some TV drama
attention grabbing epitome
of cloddish huff.

            —*The New York Times* Crossword, 2/16/18

Self-Portrait Redacted

Male white
pleasure to serve
please schedule a follow up

Former smoker lutein
Claritin fish oil Van
no lab results

Coronary
pulmonary
preoperative dysfunction

Screening for
health disease
degenerative sleep.

      —WestMed physical exam report, April 24, 2017.

Laurel S. Peterson

The Fermi Paradox

The father of the first nuclear reactor
estimated extraterrestrials could indeed come visit,
but we haven't heard from any.
Maybe no advanced civilization has
lasted long enough to explore other galaxies
or protect its peace.
Might we also be rushing towards
our own fateful midnight?

—Yann Verdo, "Enrico Fermi To Elon Musk, An Eternal Search For Life On (And Off) Earth," *Les Echos*, Jan. 22, 2018, English edition, *Worldcrunch*.

Dear Beloved

I have sent you e-mail lately
without no feedback from you
in regards to the favorable endeavor.
Its a very sensitive task and I will like
to discuss this issues with you briefly,
which I believe we could both accomplish
this mutual benefit within few days
before I past to the Ghost,
due to my deteriorating ailment but first
I will need swift response from you
on this matter before I proceed further,
contact me via email,
for more exclusive details await you.

      —Gina Xing <pengshekmo1@gina.com
      Mar 7 at 6:52 PM
      To: laurelpeterson@att.net

Classification

Drawn with a very fine camel-hair brush,
the water from a long way off
looks like Saturday afternoons we spent
walking in woods and rough places.
Latin binomials grew relationships.
Whatever faults Man may have,
diversity, offspring,
frame the world.
On my hill, diverted,
the common dayflower
confesses
in showy blue petals.

—Sue Hubbell, *A Country Year: Living the Questions*, Mariner Books 1999.

The Deification of Food

Twenty-five courses, a five hour service, one bite each:
apple cider aspic around pheasant sliver,
offered on oak leaf, oak twig flamed
the moment it's served
to perfume the air with autumn's incense.

Five million North Koreans face famine.
Invaded by cinch bugs,
wireworms, grubs, maggots—
moist and white like eyes with no pupil—
summer's maize rotted.

How can any sensible eater—
aerated foie, pickled beet, mashad plum, brioche—
compare that simply transcendent cheeseburger
with the lapidary perfection of French Laundry—
MARCHO FARM "JOUES DE VEAU":
Green Asparagus, Jidori Hen Egg,
"Pain de Campagne" and Spanish Capers—
or the genre-bending inventiveness of WD-50?
Appetizer: Cuttlefish, cashew, rootbeer, watercress 19

We want the peak
of sensation on the palate
to be all
you feel.

TASTING MENU: 140 WINE PAIRING: 85
We ask that the entire table participate in the tasting menu.

At least 40 people died in northern Kenya,
their cattle, camels and donkeys failing
next to them. Think of the stench.
MOULARD DUCK "FOIE GRAS EN TERRINE":
Duck "Confit," Cornichon,
Pear Relish,
Frisée and Dijon Mustard
(30.00 supplement)

PRIX FIXE 270.00 | SERVICE INCLUDED

Five years of drought:
no crops, no food for animals,
nothing growing anywhere.
Ground cracked like glass
in every direction,
cracks big enough to swallow
your majestic Manolos or regal Guccis.
ROYAL OSSETRA CAVIAR
Savoy Cabbage "Velouté,"
Knell's Mangalitsa Ham, Potato "Mille Feuille"
and French Laundry Garden Radishes
(50.00 supplement)

One billion suffer from hunger:
mostly babies, their bellies bloated
like jellyfish, and mothers
who pray for men to feed them.
100 million more than two years ago—
that's four thousand times around the earth
in a line, a lonely communion of one person per mile,
with no food and a few grey threads on her back—
because the bankers, real estate agents, mortgage brokers
in your neighborhood lured you to sign
on the dotted line for that variable rate mortgage—
just one bite of the apple never harmed anyone—
so they could worship at Daniel, Le Bernardin,
Alinea, Chez Panisse,
kneel before Hermes and Birkin,
sport their Movado.

What's your recipe for perfect toast?
Krug. Dom Perignon. Veuve Clicquot.
PRIX FIXE 270.00 | VICE INCLUDED

—Menu entries from WD-50 and The French Laundry. News from *BBC World News* and *CNN Online*.

Marian O'Brien Paul

Beware

Acrobatic hunters
voracious . . .
Black-chinned hummingbird
dangling from red plastic feeder like
stray Christmas ornament
In a state of torpor?
regenerating its batteries before
dropping down, flying off?
Hanging not by feet but
by its head in the grip
of a three-inch long
green praying
mantis
Mantis clinging with back legs
to rim of the feeder
holding feathered catch in
seemingly reverent front legs
chewing through hummingbird's
skull to get the brain tissue within
Standard sequence:
insects feed on plants
or one another, and then
birds hunt down insects
But carnivorous mantises
prey on hummingbirds and
other small-to-middling birds
more than most people realize . . . .

—Natalie Angier, "Birds Beware: The Praying Mantis Wants Your Brain," *The New York Times*, September 22, 2017.

Turkish Face-lifts

High school fall term—
Darwin conspicuously absent;
elementary school teachers will
promote jihad as "love of homeland"
The image of Mustafa Kemal Ataturk
(created modern secular Turkish state,
1923) is plastered everywhere. References
in schools to Ataturk to be downgraded
In a country long polarized between
religious majority and secular elites
the overhaul of 170 curriculum topics:
a frontal assault on fragile tradition
A tense time: Erdogan's crackdown
on opponents which new curriculum
lauds as "legendary, heroic," no less
than a revolution to alter education
assure conservative, religious view
prevails. Erdogan feels religion was
marginalized for decades. This is
his revenge: firing 33,000 teachers
closing scores of schools. The new
curriculum underplays Ataturk's
contribution to Turkey. Jihad in
Turkish translate[s] to "violent and
political struggle." Hay Eytan Cohen
Yanarocak said the new changes show
"Turkey is changing direction and is
no longer, by default, a Western state."

—Dan Bilefsky,"In Turkey's New Curriculum, Ataturk, Darwin, and Jihad Get Face-Lifts," *The New York Times*, September 18, 2017.

I Say to You, God is Everywhere

Our annual parish picnic
great day for our community
the weather glorious, perfect
We're so glad you're here;
all are welcome
More routine activities:
gathering the youth group
starting Sunday classes
renewing our ministries
looking for new leaders
Volunteers
visionaries reach for the stars
Unsung heroes over 150 years
brought our parish together
Planning ahead – way ahead
is critical: St. Thomas the Apostle
Catholic Church, Hyde Park
celebrating God's people
in extraordinary variety
1869 - 2019

—The Sunday Bulletin for St. Thomas the Apostle Catholic Church, Hyde Park,
Chicago, Illinois, September 17, 2017.

Future: Moving Backward

City center Ankara, bronze statue
of young woman reading:
"Human Rights Monument"
I, college student in 1990, we
drinking beer, smoking, listening
rock music, clack of backgammon pieces
bars, teahouses: Opposite worlds
East and West
traditions and modernity
religion and secularism –
confusing to outsiders
but we Turks didn't mind
Over years, monument earned
political reputation – government
repression of Kurdish-majority areas
Denied: equal rights, education
in mother tongue . . . activists rally
at Human Rights Monument, issue
Press statements. Others followed:
secularists, Turkish religious sects,
women's rights groups,
sexual minorities . . .
Coup attempt July 2016
more than 200 dead
Traumatized: entire nation
Erdogan declared state of emergency
initiated vast purge – 150,000 expelled from jobs
50,000 arrested. Crackdown especially harsh
for journalists, writers, intellectuals
Media outlets shut down, Wikipedia banned
journalists imprisoned, blacklisted, academics
fired, detained, stigmatized, demonized
two committed suicide
Under rule of law everyone is innocent
until proven guilty. In Turkey, now
the opposite: people baselessly charged
expected to prove their innocence
Iconic opposition newspaper Cumhuriyet
editors, accused-conspirators in coup

Protests, sit-ins around
Human Rights Monument
Nuriye Gulmen, literature professor
Semih Ozaka, who taught primary school
—expelled from jobs—on hunger strike
Police dispersed sit-in, detained supporters
barricaded area. Gulman, Ozakca in jail
Citizens support hunger strikers
singing songs and anthems
Ankara banned
Trajectory shows fragility of democracy:
delicate ecosystem of checks and balances needs
free media, conscious civil society
to survive . . .
Elite under Erdogan assume
majority in ballot box gives
legitimacy, power to do
whatever they please
It doesn't
Democracy requires
separation of powers
rule of law
a free press
academic freedom:
all broken in Turkey
Lifestyle under siege
secularism chipped away
one million students enrolled
in imam-hatip schools to train imams
Turkey:
more religious
more paranoid
more inward-looking
Demise of Turkey's democracy shows
history doesn't necessarily move forward
Sometimes, it goes backward

—Elif Safak, "Turkey's Future Is Moving Backward," *The New York Times*,
September 19, 2017.

Clarence Wolfshohl

After the Eclipse

For Sale:

Orion Sky Quest
8" Telescope,

many extras,

carrying case
for extras

&
owner's manuals.

Sky Wizard
2
Star Finder,
$600.

For more details
email:

xanadu.1
@earthlink.net

—from the Classifieds

Each Generation Discovers
in response to a found poem in a college literary journal

Each generation discovers f**k anew.
Perhaps in a funk and wag'n all of slang
of the time or in the cult novel read
behind the math text in a last period
algebra class. Remember Holden?

Each generation looks f**k up
in the unabridged Webster's and points
it out to buddies—a camaraderie
of the dirty word—the jabs on the arm,
the elbow in the side, and snot-sucking snickers.

Oh, what a celebration
to see f**k in print,
as if our youthful intensity
willed it to create itself
within those musty pages,
as if our adults
were too dumb to find
the word in a world
all too much in need.

Jennifer Glick

Threshold

to feel somehow
touched everywhere
by emptiness and a
chance to walk
this curious moment
breathing the world
becoming a center
unfolding
where one lifts entire trees
into the stars

—John Landretti, "Nameless Season: On the Wonder and Wisdom of Ambiguity,"
ORION Magazine, March/April 2016.

Present, Be

stare
at the wide open nothingness, close up
questions don't matter
answers without questions
find the beauty
of innocence and experience
and rest

—Leanne Shapton, Agnes Martin's "Summer, 1964." *The New York Times Magazine*, October 8, 2017.

Michelle Hartman

Irony
for Leigh Washburn

devout, Muslim friend
who knows me well
well enough to know
I'm a practicing
Mahayana Buddhist
sent a Christmas card

the front a picture
of a stained glass
Mary and Joseph
the Christ child

'Silent Night,
    Holy Night'

the inside says
 "May the wonders
     and the blessings of this
   Holy Season
remain in your heart
throughout the coming year."

nice sentiments
   Islam and Buddhist
      alike can get behind
   "wonders and blessings"

I think
but should we
carouse this way
in a third-party's
neighborhood?

on the back of the card
it was made in China...

probably by some nice
Buddhist ladies
from the adjacent village

—An email from Leigh Washburn, my first teacher in Buddhism.

for the courtier and the lover

to draw attention of the queen
perform well in that masculine arena—
    tension between desire and ambition
    beating the air above her—
tilting war with masculine conceit
    desire
he loses control in arenas of imperialism
    governance and war
    successful courtiership
resents prizes lost
    aristocratic conventions
and practices of erotic desire
    drain the masculine ambition
he depends on grace and favor

long live the king

—Emily Mayne, "Love Poetry in Renaissance England." In *Disenchanted and Disgruntled*, Lamar University Literary Press.

James Finnegan

Forward-looking statements

are provided to allow potential investors the opportunity
to understand
management's beliefs and opinions in respect
of the future
so that they may use such beliefs
and opinions
as one factor in evaluating an investment.

These statements are not guarantees of future performance
and undue
reliance should not be placed on them.
Such forward-looking
statements necessarily involve known and unknown
risks and uncertainties,
which may cause actual performance
and financial results
in future periods to differ materially
from any projections
of future performance or result
expressed or implied
by such forward-looking statements.

—https://corporatefinanceinstitute.com/resources/templates/transactions
/forward-looking-statements-example/

Cory Sisterhenm

Everything is Probably Not Fine

History: mostly no recent trauma
Comparison: None.
Findings:
Bones: Unremarkable. No acute abnormalities.
Unremarkable.
Unremarkable.
None.
Impression: Negative.

—Personal Medical Document

Animal Consciousness

Animals have minds
beings have always empathized with beings
serious effort to understand the minds of others.
Xenophobic humans are not
creatures different from us.
Other experiences have dimmed,
and our pets now read us much better than we read them.
Derailed by some very influential thinkers,
the physical body is merely a machine with mechanical motion?
Our human bodies house the ghost in the machine
Without consciousness or feelings.
The fox caught in a trap cries in pain,
but what we hear,
is evidence of pain,
it is the sound of damaged machinery.
A reason for our slow search has been manifest.
Data could not be considered legitimate inquiry.
Ignored; ergo it did not exist.
Convincing to sensitive observers,
Animal experiences.
Pleasures of many sorts:
moods, fear, sexual feelings, hunger, confusion,
agitation, aggressive urges, anger, pain.
Intuitions tell us that we have these experiences.
With great energy,
the essence of being alive is not biological process,
but every animal's tiny niche.
Adapt, avoid pain, seek pleasure.
Being is to *experience*,
moment by moment,
to think, feel, fear, hope, dream, plan ahead, remember the good things,
and all.
The hummingbird, the otter, the deer
all animals can suffer
be grounded.
The sphere of moral concern
is also one of the bases.
(Non-hurtfulness).

—James Lee Christian, *An Introduction to the Art of Wondering*, Harcourt Brace College Publishers, 1994.

A Tree Grows in China
devouring the countryside

this wind-blown hill
could be described as profoundly inspiring,
deeply strange.
For miles
the earth is dun-colored
dry, stubbled yellow grass. The
hillsides
emblazoned with
geometric shapes
striped with bands
standing in rigid formation
a display
how barren
this place.
Desert landscape dotted.
"See?" he says.
Vast tracts of
pure desert
partly to blame,
the main culprit
the number of people.

—Vince Beiser, "China's Crazy Plan to Keep Sand From Swallowing the World,"
Mother Jones, September/October 2017.

Joseph Bathanti

Compliments of North Carolina Correction Enterprises

- Signs and License Plates
- Lubricating Products
- Clothing and Linens
- Draperies
- Upholstered Furniture
- Reupholstery Services
- Janitorial Products
- Metal and Stainless Steel Items
- Antifreeze
- Traffic Paints
- Printing and Duplicating
- Wood Furniture
- Manpower Service

Tom Nicotera

Found Poem #1

Copies Now
Future Kids
Human Elements

    3 businesses listed on a sign in a lobby.

Found Poem #2

Do you feel better, worse, or about the same?
Press: 1) For getting better
          2) About the same
          3) Getting worse
          4) If you are unsure

    Telemarketing phone message.

Al's Lament

My friend Tom died about an hour ago.
There is a full moon at the ferry landing tonight.
I'll get a coffee and sit there listening
to Tom's favorite radio station.
Just came back from the library to see
a documentary about the young Francesca Woodman
who is now a famous photographer
but committed suicide at 22 years
because her art was not taken seriously as art.
She wrote a journal that was part of the film script
as well as interviews from family and friends.
I did that because I knew today that Tom
was on morphine, and his daughter says
he won't make it through the day.
Sad. All I can think of is my mom
on morphine in a quiet room with a small candle.
I was all alone with her just looking at how
peaceful she was as her tear ducts
kept watering and finally
she took her last breath.

—Lines arranged, with his permission, from an email by my friend, Al Lepore, Nov. 29, 2012. "Al's Lament" was published in *What Better Place to Be Than Here?* Foothills Publishing, 2015.

Janet Kuypers

found poem

this is the law,
we follow the law,
and I will begin doing that
tomorrow

—Final comments from Rod Blagojevic (Illinois Governor) in a statement before leaving for a 14-year jail sentence, heard on the news & written 3/14/12. Originally published in cc&d magazine (http://scars.tv/ccd) v237.

found haiku

Himmler wanted the
Ahnenerbe to prove Jesus
wasn't a Jew.

—Originally published in cc&d magazine (http://scars.tv/ccd) v261 and *Down in the Dirt* magazine (http://scars.tv/dirt) v151

quoting twitter with a found haiku

What will save us from
isis? Water with fluoride,
vaccines, fewer guns?

—Originally published in *Down in the Dirt Magazine* (http://scars.tv/dirt) v133 and the cc&d magazine (http://scars.tv/ccd)

'One of the Most Hated Women in America'

she keeps a lonely,
guarded life now
in her words,
"I was in confinement
for twenty-three hours a day
for weeks at a time."
in her words,
"My sentence was doled out
long before there was a verdict.
Sentence first, verdict afterward."
Guilty long before a day in court."
in her words,
she does not have a
"significant problem
with not telling the truth."
in her words,
"I hate to say this, but
cops believe other cops,
cops tend to victimize the victims.
I see why I was treated
the way I was even
had I been completely truthful."
"Cops lie to people every day.
I'm just one of the
unfortunate idiots
who admitted they lied."
in her words,
"I don't give a shit
about what anyone
thinks about me,
I never will.
I'm OK with myself.
I sleep pretty good at night."

—Words spoken by Casey Anthony since the 2008 death of her infant daughter
Caylee. Originally published in cc&d magazine (http://scars.tv/ccd) v276

Chantel Langlinais Carlson

The Night Stalker

Maybe you have to have a brush
with death before you can really reflect

on life—on the people and times
that really meant something to you,

like childhood, dreams of sailing
on silver seas and wooden shoes,

visions of sugar plums dancing.
Silver seas, sugar plums.

The visions, the nightmares of a child
are perhaps the most frightening

and horrifying. Some people
who were in Chicago during

the first stifling hot weeks of July
would say that were so

if they were still alive.

—"Kolchak: The Night Stalker – Episode 9: Spanish Moss Murders." Synopsis on Fandom.

Lake Martin

This lake—
a mossy green dollop
surrounded by thin
trees and cypress trunks—

serves as a wonderful,
easily accessible
introduction to bayou
landscapes. A few walking paths,

as well as a boardwalk,
take visitors over
the mirror-reflection
sheen of the swamp

while overhead thousands
of great and cattle egrets
and blue herons perch
in haughty indifference.

—"Lake Martin: Bird Sanctuary in Cajun Wetlands," from lonelyplanet.com

Jennifer Kidney

Fortune Cookie Poems

Number 1

Most people spend their lives
reading the menu
instead of enjoying the banquet.

You may attend a party
where strange customs prevail.

Hope for the best,
but prepare for the worst.

You love sports, horses, and gambling,
but not to excess.

You long to see the great pyramids in Egypt.

The important thing is
to express yourself.

Your native wit should be your fortune.

Number 2

To most people
nothing is more troublesome
than thinking.

Remember,
birds are entangled by their feet
and men by their tongues.

Fortune does not change men:
it unmasks them.

You will have to stay awake
to make your dreams come true.

A friend is a present
you give to yourself.

News of an old sweetheart
who still thinks much of you.

Accept the next proposition you hear.

Number 3

You find beauty in ordinary things;
do not lose this ability.

Your emotional nature is
strong and sensitive.

You will live to a ripe old age
happy in the love and respect
of many children.

Like the river flows into the sea
some things are just meant to be.

Susan King

Full of Sleep

Rain poured down in sheets,
ran in wide, watery fishtails
off the edges of roofs.
Phostis closed the wooden shutter
to the little slit
window in his cell.
With it open things
were about as wet
inside as they were
out in the storm.
But with it closed,
the bare square room
was dark as night;
fitfully flickering lamps
did little to cut the gloom.
After a few days
of the steady rain,
he felt as full of sleep
as a new wineskin
is of wine.

—Harry Turtledove, *Krispos of Videssos*, Del Ray, 1991.

William Virgil Davis

Consider the momentous

event

in architecture when

the wall

p a r t e d

and the

c

o

l

u

m

n

became.

—Louis I. Kahn

The mind is too narrow
to contain itself entirely.

Where is that part of it
which it does not itself
contain?

—Saint Augustine

I wrote this poem
before I knew how
to write poems.

—Undergraduate student in a Creative Writing class

What is a poet?

An unhappy person
who conceals

profound anguish
in his heart

but whose lips
are so formed

that as sighs
and cries

pass over them
they sound

like beautiful
music.

—Søren Kierkegaard

I am an ignorant man,

almost a poet.

—George Santayana

J.S. Dennis

A Matter of God's Principles

The uncertainty principle
        had profound
               implications
for the way
     in which
        we
  view
            the world.
Even after
     more
         than
      fifty years

   they   have   not   been

    fully

appreciated
      by many   philosophers
             and are
still
      the subject
          of much
   controversy.

The uncertainty   principle
     signaled
       an end
to the dream
    of   a   theory   of
            science,
       a model
of   the   universe
    that would   be

completely
deterministic:
one
certainly
cannot
predict
future
events
exactly
if one
cannot
even
measure
the present
state
of the
universe
precisely!

We could
still
imagine
that there
is
a set of
laws
that
determines
events
completely
for
some
supernatural
being,
who could
observe
the present
state
of the universe
without disturbing
it.

However,
such
models
of
the
universe
are not
of
much
interest

to

us

ordinary   mortals.

It seems   better

to

employ

the   principle

of   economy

known as

Occam's

Razor

and cut

out

all

the   features

of

the

theory

that

cannot

be

observed.

—Stephen W. Hawking, *A Brief History of Time*, Bantam Books, 1988.

A Parlor Game

The girl hesitates to drink,
her fingers approaching the glass
as she smiles at the soldier's remarks;
the woman, by contrast, drains her glass.
Are the soldier and the gentleman,
neither of whom is drinking,
using alcohol as a means of seduction?
Is this a game designed to test
the partner's resistance?
Or is it merely theatre,
perhaps in a rehearsal in which
the characters are not yet at ease?
This would explain the elusiveness
of their behavior, the awkwardness
of the poses, the illusory character
of the emotions—
not action but its imitation.

—Pierre Cabanne, *Vermeer*, Editions Terrail, 2004.

Mere Chatter about Shelley

Partly
    Protestant Reformation
and partly
    French Revolution,
the critical revolution
    swept through literary studies
like measles
    through a primitive tribe,
demonstrating with ease
    the emptiness of the old order
demystifying
    and "emptying
out" its unsupported
    humanistic beliefs.

—Alvin Kernan, *The Death of Literature*, Yale University Press, 1990.

A Philosophical Commentary on the Need to Define the Dialectical Equivocations of Anti-Scientism as Reflections on the Rise of Bioethical Metonymic Rationalism in the Early Twenty-first Century: To Wit:

Bullshit
           is unavoidable
                                        whenever   circumstances
                     require
someone to talk
                                without knowing
      what
                           he is
                                                  talking
        about.

Thus the   production   of
                    bullshit
                            is stimulated
                                            whenever
      a   person's
                                       obligations
or opportunities
                     to speak
                             about
some
                        topic
                                           exceed
his knowledge
                  of the facts
                                         relevant
      to   that   topic.

This discrepancy
                   is common
      in   public   life,
           where people
                  are frequently

impelled—

by their own   propensities

or the demands

of

others—

to speak

about matters

of which

they are

ignorant.

Closely related instances

arise

from   the

wide-

spread

conviction

that it is

the

responsibility

of a citizen

in a democracy

to have   opinions

about

every-

thing,

or at least

every-

thing

that pertains

to the conduct

of his country's

affairs.

The lack of   any

significant

connection

between

a person's

opinions

and   his

                              apprehension

                 of

                    reality

           will   be

even more   severe,

                        needless to say,

       for

                     someone

          who believes it   his

    responsibility,

as a

      conscientious

              moral   agent,

               to evaluate

events

         and   conditions

in   all   parts

                         of

      the

          world.

The contemporary

         proliferation of

                      bullshit

   also

     has

        deeper

            sources.

—Harry G. Frankfurt, *On Bullshit*, Princeton University Press, 2005.

To Lady Cynthia Asquith

We have lived a few days on the seashore,
with the wave banging up at us.
Also over the river, beyond the ferry,
there is the flat silvery world,
as in the beginning, untouched:
with pale sand, and very much white foam,
row after row, coming from under the sky,
in the silver evening:
and no people, no people at all,
no houses, no buildings, only a haystack
on the edge of the shingle,
and an old black mill.
For the rest, the flat unfinished world
running with foam and noise
and silvery light, and a few gulls
swinging like a half-born thought.
It is a great thing to realise
that the original world is still there
—perfectly clean and pure...

—*The Letters of D.H. Lawrence*, The Viking Press, 1932.

Gregory Ellis

The Life of the Law Has Not Been Logic

The life of the law has not been logic.
Has been experience,
the felt necessities of the time,
moral and political theories,
intuitions of public policy,
even prejudices,
more than syllogism,
in determining rules
by which men be governed.

Law embodies the story
of a nation's development,
and cannot be dealt with as only
axioms
and corollaries
of mathematics.

To know what it is,
we must
know what it has been,
and tends to become,
must consult history
and existing theories of legislation but,
most difficult,
understand the combination of the two
into new products.

The substance of law
at any given time
nearly corresponds with
what is then understood convenient;

but its form and machinery,

and degree of desired results,

depend much upon
its past.

—Oliver Wendell Holmes, Jr., *The Common Law*, Little, Brown, and Company 1881.

Congress Shall Make No Law

Persecution for the expression of opinions.
To me,
perfectly logical.
If you have no doubt of your premises or power
and want certain result with all your heart,
you naturally express your wishes in law
and sweep away all opposition.

To allow opposition by speech
seems
you think the speech impotent,
or do not care whole-heartedly for the result,
or doubt either your power or premises.

But when men have realized that time upset
many fighting faiths,
they may come to believe
the ultimate good desired
better reached by
free trade in ideas,
the best test of truth
the power of the thought
to get accepted,
and truth
the only ground upon which their wishes
safely can be carried out.

That,
at any rate
is the theory of our Constitution,
an experiment as all life is.
Every year
if not every day
we wager our salvation upon some prophecy
based upon imperfect knowledge.

While that experiment is part of our system,
we should be eternally vigilant against attempts
to check expression of opinions we loathe
and believe fraught with death,
unless they so imminently threaten
the pressing purposes of the law
that immediate check
is required.

Only the emergency
that makes it immediately dangerous
to leave correction of
evil counsels
to time
warrants any exception to the sweeping command,
"Congress shall make
no law abridging
the freedom of speech."

—The dissent of Justice Oliver Wendell Holmes, Jr. in Adams v. United States
(1919) 250 U.S. 616.

Jamie Stern

Small Whistles

Used in ceremonies
The sound of the whistles
Believed to represent
The voices of supernatural beings.
Small whistles
Concealed in the dancer's mouth

—Display about the Haida tribe at the American Museum of Natural History.

Capturing Diseases

The Haida believed that diseases were caused
By the intrusion of some
Supernatural object
Or by a person's
Losing his soul.

In curing rites,
A shaman danced, sang,
Captured the patient's wandering soul
With a hollow bone tube.

A soul catcher.

Sometimes the shaman used
A soul catcher
To blow disease away.
Or accompany war parties
To kill the souls of the enemy.

—Display about the Haida tribe at the American Museum of Natural History.

Nathan Lewis

Hartford Nietzsche Drawing

To live alone one must be beast or god
says Aristotle. Leaving out
the 3rd possibility. ONE   MUST   BE   BOtH.

Name *Nombre*   Year I was born *Año en que naci*
son of a preacher man   Oct. 15th, 1844

    —Paper tags at the Wadsworth Athenaeum in Hartford, Connecticut, that invite viewers to draw or comment on art seen in the museum (meant for kids).

Hartford Self

PAINTING IS A PRIVATE
   Love Affair.

Name *Nombre*   Year I was born *Año en que naci*
NaThAn LeWiS   what year it now

    —Paper tags at the Wadsworth Athenaeum in Hartford, Connecticut, that invite viewers to draw or comment on art seen in the museum (meant for kids).

Whitman Is Street

1344   Failing to fetch me at first keep encou ged
1345   Missing me one place sear
1346   I stop

COPS
LIE.

somewhere waiting for you.

—From an Instagram posting

Phrases Found in Dreams

CHOKE ON THE
STRINGS OF MY
   KITE

I laugh at myself
Then you laugh at me
Not made.

Laura Altshul

Atlantic Flyway

Every autumn, tens of thousands
pass through the city, some by day
some by night, responding to hidden cues:
insects, birds, and bats
over enormous bodies of water
through entire weather systems
to extreme corners of the continent
and beyond.
Smallest hummingbirds, bald eagles,
neotropical songbirds, oceangoing seabirds—
mass movement winging southbound.

Among the hordes, hawks prey
on fellow travelers:
falcons, open air speedsters
with scythe-like wings, blackened eyes;

sharp-shinned hawks,
secretive and shy,
choose dense woodlands
for nesting, use short powerful wings
to weave past obstacles;
long tails counterbalance
sharp turns and
high speed bloody ambushes,
knifing through clear open spaces –
strong wing beats
intersperse with graceful gliding:
flap, flap, flap... glide
riding the wide-open winds southbound.

Wave of migrants
moving through the city.

—"Remarkable, Ancient Journey," *The New York Times*, October 22, 2017.

Still Awaiting Trial in Alabama, Kharon Davis Writes

I wake to... doors clicking and keys clinking;
deputies... retrieve my blanket at 5:00 am.
Up and alert, stretching my legs, getting ready
to take off on my one hour jog – in place.
A guard or inmate asks where
am I running to? I reply Home.

All day long all I do is exercise,
read, and pace the floor –
an animal stuck in a cage.
Locked in segregated confinement.
No matter the size of this bouldered burden
laid on my back, I'm a bona fide soldier
 until my oppressors set me free.

This jail will make you feel like a nobody,
like you're better off dead.
I'd not seen my mother for over 2 years;
she and the NAACP had to...see...the sheriff
to be approved a ten minute visit.
Awakened to this unannounced blessing,
I couldn't believe the beautiful face
across from me through plexiglass,
and shared tears of joy with my Queen.

But 4 guards and a lieutenant came,
forced me next door
with handcuffs and tazers
without reason.

When the cell door closed, I immediately knew
what they were insinuating: Kill Yourself.

It really doesn't matter what someone thinks,
you've got to be self-willed and determined
to believe in yourself.

—"Justice Delayed: 10 Years in Jail," *The New York Times*, September 19, 2017.

Missing the Trees

Iceland: austere, largely
treeless landscapes,
punctuated by vast glaciers,
and stark volcanoes.

Viking settlers took axes
to Iceland's once-vast
birch forests
over a thousand years ago.
Soil eroded.
Volcanic ash blew,
fell and settled.

Now
strong winds, sandstorms
blast paint off cars.

Now
with flats of saplings
and red planting tool
a foot soldier fights
to reforest Iceland
to bring new life
to barren land –
this cold, wind-blown
inhospitable
once-fertile
soil.

 —"Vikings Razed the Forests. Will They Regrow?" *The New York Times*, October
22, 2017.

Loretta Diane Walker

Lessons From Night's Visit

night
walked and
jumped

moved with
an unexpected yearning to
sit at a table with my family

on the table's surface
a freshly
cooked meal

night gathered around me
our hands folded on top of our heads
a vocabulary for friendship

I've learned
what it   means to be
family

a year
contains a lot of contradictions
strengthens   in new ways

climbing
is a confrontation of morality and an
adventure that makes me feel

I've learned   that grass
smells great and wind feels
amazing and rain is a miracle
earth,

a swirl of chaos and conflict,
is beautiful

—Scott Kelly, "What I Learned in Space," *AARP*, October/November 2017.

Trilogy on Seasons

i

Fall is
an event.
A gorgeous movie.
A salute to
art.
A gift
like the wings of a bird.

ii

The year is racing towards
   winter.
Where does it want to be? It raged its way through
autumn
without stopping for breath.
Blackbirds
stopped singing.

iii

There is indecision before   winter. Plants die.
Turn vibrant colors.
Relieved of hot summers and terrified of the
long winter ahead,
we celebrate and mourn the green times
behind us.
Seasons split into
words.
Splintered, winter comes
littered with scraps of
autumn.

—i. Amy S. Eckert and Christina Ianzito, "Heartland Getaways," *AARP*, October/November 2017. ii. Press Association. "Early signs of autumn already appearing in natural world, *the guardian*. Web. Tuesday, 1 July 2014. iii. Dan Nosowitz, "Why Does the Season Before Winter Have Two Names? A Look at the History of Fall and Autumn," *Atlas Obscura*. Web. Tuesday, 3 November 2017.

Scars

I have scars on my face
      because I played.
I have scars on my hands
      because I rescued.
I have scars on my heart
      because I loved.
And the scars are a beautiful life.

—Walker, Vonnie, Tucker. Facebook Post. 9 November.

Joanie DiMartino

Officially She Didn't

there is one log of the Morgan
girls who went to sea with their husbands
she could take the sun and work up a position
a little piano in between the two doors in the after cabin
preferred to staying home alone
spent a lot of time helping to navigate the ship
she certainly knew she was going on a whaler
your mother was rated as a navigator aboard the *Morgan*
Yes
bringing out tea when they had the gamming
did your mother like the sea
in my mother's handwriting
her keeping one of the logs
my mother downstairs looking at the chronometers
I remember my mother
there wasn't much to do at sea
that's why she took up navigation

—Mystic Seaport Museum Oral Interview with James Earle, 9/16/1974. He sailed
as a child with his father, Captain Earle, and his mother, Honor Earle, said to be
assistant navigator, on the Charles W. Morgan whaling bark in the early 1900s.

Oysters

I have read, which suits me
best of anything. I am the only
female in the bay, shame
is felt here—actions
are so public—have passed
the day in my room reading
with some writing.

We had just got a large pan
of oysters
on the table when a boat
came alongside. I retired
in my room when the french
Captain took my place
and the Oysters
did not last long. When I
left the cabin, alas upon
enquiry, oysters
were pau as the natives
say, which is ended
or gone—

Morning. Rain, light
fog. Oranges and sweet
lemons which my husband
purchased this forenoon
I have been putting up
in hopes they keep.

Towards night a boat
was very badly stoven.
After tea found
such was the case: one
poor man was never
seen after the whale struck
the boat, he must
have been killed by the whale.

My husband has concluded
to whale no more,
which has left us much alone.

—Joan Druett, editor. *She Was a Sister Sailor: Mary Brewster's Whaling Journals 1845-1851,* (February, 1847), Mystic Seaport Museum, Mystic, CT: 1992.

All Alone Taking Oil Fast?

Might we anticipate?

The question is, do we feel thankfull
to God for his kind and watchfull care over us?

I would think sometimes
we are all here now--but where
will we be the next hour?

Where are you, pray?

What if I had remained
at home? Yes, the 4 of July has agane passed,
and how think you love I have spent
the day? And why, have I done my duty?

But under present circumstances,
what am I to do? How can I write of it?

But what has become of Henry H.,
and all of our good friends in America?
And pray what would the reality
occasion? Can I realize it?

Oh, blessed hope, what is not religion worth?

What can I think of myself,
sitting with my hands folded and apparrently
thinking--that I am to be carried
to heaven on flowery beds of ease?

Oh how often I think of you in your quiet
little room, and if I was there to give
it a good brush now and then,
would it not be pleasanter?

But what is the use of letting the crosses
and vanities of this life intrude
upon the hours set apart

for the service of God?

But what shall I do
without you? Oh, Edwin, how can I
longer wait your return?

To whom much is given of him much
will be required, but does that lessen
the obligation of the steward
who possesses the one tallent?
Christopher, will you
get me one?

Have I lived as though I expected
to meet my Father there? For why not
praise and adore him here
as we shall in heaven?

When shall we ever get any where
where we want to?

Some times I feel very unhappy,
at other times I think
would this have been my situation
had it been contriary
to my Husband's wishes?

She knows her husband
would wish it   therefore
why should she hesitate?

Oh Dear what next?

Dear Children, who would do for them
as their parents? What better are they
than the poor heathen,
especially hear at sea? Why did I leave

her at home?

How could I have endured it?

But she is gone,
and my sweet Child where are you?
Is it not useualy darkest
just before day?

When oh when
will you come, my love?

—Anne MacKay, editor. *She Went A-Whaling: the Journal of Martha Smith Brewer Brown from Orient, Long Island, New York, Around the World on the Whaling Ship Lucy Ann, 1847-1849*, Oysterponds Historical Society, Orient, NY, 1993.

sauced & scoused

for a pleasure   gastronomic

bold   samples   duff

& plum   step into

    a brandied tavern

twice-past pickled

    present   your tongue

raised & baked

    and fricasseed

island oysters   squeezed

and shucked   tack hard

    past temperance union

twice   light-relished

    present   your tongue

    —"A Taste of History: 19th-Century Foods of Mystic Seaport" recipe booklet, menu insert, 1996.

Amie E. Reilly

Tea to One

visiting Europe took a liking to
America, where
it has remained popular ever since.

actually, 14 different sizes
still in common use today
are especially small
and a few
are built in different sizes, each uses
the same fingerlings, allowing
transfer
with ease.

invented to be a bridge
between sections,
and to boost the
military, The
combination of metal body and wood
allows it to blend equally well
However
classified
its
system

Today,
occasionally They are
solo

ALT SURVIVAL KIT
_holder   _soft, clean cloth
_pencil   _extra
_music   _book

—"The E flat Alto Saxophone," Bruce Pearson, *Standard of Excellence: Enhanced book one: Alto Saxophone*, Neil A. Kjos Music Company, 1993.

Gay Paluch

Dear Grandpa and Grandma,

Having quite the experience at Basic Training
yet to determine
good or bad
doing cool things:
shooting M-4's   marching   field maneuvers   obstacle courses
low-crawling through fire ant hills
stung all over my forearms, my belly, my eyebrow
(that sucked!)
scored 33/40 on my rifle qualification test
nothing comes naturally
have to work hard on everything
a lot to remember
start training with grenades next week
(I'm nervous, to be honest!)

A few good friends here
one letting me use his phone
to talk to my lady friend in the Ukraine
(yes, you read that right!)
she loves God and children
wants help with English
is teaching me Russian
I hope to get her over here sometime.

Georgia is too hot, way too humid.
Why do places like this exist on Earth?
Why do we Americans end up fighting in the Middle East,
the armpit of the planet?
Can't we fight someplace a little cooler
for once, (or can we not fight at all!)
Thanks for your letter and support.
I'll see you soon.

—A letter from our 20 year old grandson written during the early stages of basic
training at Ft. Benning GA, July 30, 2017.

In sweet silence before sunrise

I watch
> the round shield of moon fading
> copper to brass
> to whitish silver
> a long still reflection
> across a sea of glass.

The sun approaches, a red orb
> in insufferable glory
> burns, sets dew
> to twinkling, sparkling
> in a thousand rainbows
> rays rejoicing over the face
> of the world.

Flowers salute me.
> Each gives me
> its color   its grace   its perfume
> the consummation of its glory.
> From my shoulders slip
> cares, perplexities
> all griefs of existence
> leaving me with the heart
> of a little child.

Nothing beyond
> this present moment
> of innocent bliss.

—Celia Thaxter, *An Island Garden*, Houghton Mifflin, 1894.

Attempting Repentance

Columns soar amidst
richly colored stained glass
in this building created
out of disordered desires,
a monument to America's original
sins, every bishop a slaveholder.

Anniversary number 100
with no cake, no balloons
no rejoicing in this august building.
Only, seek to remedy wrongs,
grapple with the story of race,
for the sins of ancestors
are engraved in stone
and white/black lives are at stake
in violent confrontations.

Now, the bowing of heads
the whisperings of repentance
 "Lord, forgive us,
and those who came before us."

the utter silence of time.

—Julie Zaumer, *The Daily Republican*, October 14, 2017

On Deciding NOT to Choose a Flannel Shirt From the L.L. Bean Catalog

Scotch plaid in bold yarn-dyed patterns,
    Traditional fit, relaxed chest and sleeves,
Angled flap pockets, cross-stitched buttons,
    Rugged, luxurious, breathable on drizzly days,
Exclusive durability, longest wearing,
    Designed to create incredible outdoor memories,
Or cozy at homes of warmer togethers.

But, imported, all Imported, and always IMPORTED.

—"Be An Outsider," *L.L. Bean 2017 Winter Catalog.*

Vernita Hall

From a Berlin Travel Guide

There's so much in Berlin

sometimes it makes sense
to take a tour and leave

some of our favorites—
themed tours such as

"Third Reich Berlin" offers a Monday "Jewish Life" tour
visits to the concentration camp

a "Cold War" Berlin tour
about the Soviet era

firsthand accounts are a highlight all-day
tours cost €15

a "Berlin Wall" tour
costs €24, bike rental included

a truly memorable experience, WWII
normally closed to the public

Tours give you up-close views of sights
drinks, snacks, and distance

where you can sail on
through the past

can last the full circuit
with a recorded narration on headphones

for you can jump on and off
the bus driver sells tickets

the last leaves at 6 pm
most have

--"Berlin Travel Guide," *Fodor's Travel*, 11 October 2016.

Full-Day Tour of Chernobyl

*One of the most radioactively contaminated sites in the world: the
1000 mile Nuclear Power Plant (NPP) Exclusion Zone in Ukraine,
around the site of the reactor explosion of April 26, 1986.*

Low Price Guarantee!

Explore the Exclusion Zone
You are welcome to spend

maximum time inside
see an open-eye experience

Expect some changes

abandoned houses and barns
an almost fully buried village with

a kindergarten
a Red Forest

The first and worst fall-out:
the town of Pripyat

populated by 50 thousand people
before the evacuation

The fire fighters and NPP workers
badly affected by

a river of consequences
a correction point, ruins of culture

for the Prypyat youth
Ferris wheel in the amusement park

which was never open—
a disaster

After explosion:
giant catfish

<Giant secret>

Tour includes radiation
and personal departure

Necessary information
(unlikely to be confirmed):

in case of
eating, drinking, and smoking in open air
touching buildings, trees, plants
eating mushrooms, berries, fruit, and nuts
in forests of the abandoned settlements
sitting on the ground

on persons there is
a 100 percent cancellation

—"Full-Day Tour of Chernobyl and Prypiat from Kiev," *Viator*, 20 October 2016.

Tap Dance

Flint, Michigan residents can't get clean
water from their taps

The State thought it was a joke
the water started to look, smell, and taste funny

The water would come in brown
Why is the water brown?

Flint is highly corrosive
More so, turning brown

(far worse)
wasn't properly treated

(the status quo for years)
Everything was fine, toxic waste

kept in the dark
records of blood

causing near hysteria
the State is now handing out

a steady decline in population
a steady rise in crime
among the most dangerous cities
the crisis is indicative of an attitude

often just forgotten
poisoning is irreversible

There is no safe
level in a child

They deserve
because of what's happened

a state of emergency
regret   was completely avoidable

    —Sara Ganim and Linh Tran, "How tap water became toxic in Flint, Michigan," CNN, 13 Jan. 2016, 3 November 2016.

Sandra Chaff

Question #35

WHAT ARE THE NEGATIVES ABOUT YOUR NEW CAR?

I tell you, I'd prefer to have a little more   acceleration
I'm a little   big for the car
Paying for it

It's black so it always looks dirty
The back of the car looks like a bubble   and I think it's ugly
The stupid bubble in the front of the car, eats more gas than I thought

Nothing

The speedometer is on the left   I want it on the center or on the right
The trunk isn't shaped   right
The way it looks

Not driving it enough
The exhaust fumes in reverse
Seats don't go back far enough   because she is tall

The fact that it doesn't work.

—These are verbatim responses to the question "What are the Negatives About Your New Car?" selected from the *1997 J.D. Power New Car Buyer Survey.*

t. l. cummings

Round Dance

silence
scurrying feet
chatter
rhythmic drum beat

singing
burning sage
colorful shawls
dance over concrete

—Rachael White Hawk, "Idle No More," *Native Daughters Oklahoma*, 2014.

Pueblo Bonito

Only a part of the great
house still stands
because an old Indian
legend came true. A
giant slab of cliff against
which the place was built
began to lean. Centuries
of changing weather cut
deeper and deeper, while
generations of Indians
fearfully watched this
Threatening Rock.
Medicine Men believed
that when the rock fell
the world would be
embroiled in a terrible
war. Well, the huge slab
did crash down on the
village, January 22, 1941
the year of World War II
many centuries after the
Pueblo and Chaco Canyon
were abandoned.

—Betty Woods, "Pueblo Bonito," *New Mexico Magazine*, July 2017.

Power

It's 1825, and you walk
into a large Cherokee village
in northern Alabama.

Before long, you notice
   something
this bustling village

of more than 300
Native men, women
and children.

Women
   dictate the pace
     of daily life.

A Native mother
passes fry bread discs
to her children.

Another gives her slaves
directions for a day
of planting corn and tobacco.

An elderly woman
surrounded
by wide-eyed youngsters

listening intently
to the sacred
Cherokee creation story.

And then you look
to your left
and see a woman

setting her husband's
clothes

outside their home—

an unmistakable sign
she is ending
their marriage.

These are the Cherokee
 and these are their women.

—Asha Timperley, "Still Not Silent," *Native Daughters Oklahoma*, 2014.

Vivian Finley Nida

Visions
Mexico

Dead monarch butterflies carpet
a snowy forest floor in Michoacán state.
At least nine million over 40 percent of this colony,
died after an unusually intense spring storm
—possibly due to climate change—
hit their mountain sanctuary.

—"Mexico," Front Visions, *National Geographic*, September 2017.

133

Patricia Martin

Rules of Behavior

I came of age in the 60's and 70's
when all the rules about behavior
and workplaces
were different

That was the culture then.
I have since learned
it's not an excuse
in the office
or out of it
to anyone

I realized some time ago
that I needed to be a better person
and my interactions with the people
I work with
have changed

I appreciate the way
I've behaved with colleagues
in the past
has caused a lot of pain
and I sincerely apologize for it

Though I'm trying to do better
I know I have a long way to go
That is my commitment

My journey now will be
to learn about myself
and conquer my demons

—Excerpt from statement Hollywood mogul Harvey Weinstein sent to *The New York Times* responding to its exposé accusing the Hollywood mogul of decades of sexual harassment and questionable behavior toward women. *The New York Times*, October 5, 2017.

Nutella Fans Go Nuts after Discovering the Company has Secretly Changed the Formula

Marina Daydreamer said:
'#Ferrero changed the recipe for #nutella
(at least in #germany)
more sugar,
less fat
and
probably
less cocoa.

Is it the 1st of April again?'

Another social media user tweeted:
'Just heared that #Nutella changed their recipe.
I mean come on
there are things in life you CANT do!
And this is one of those things!
#sweets.'

Felien S. Geldhof added:
'They have apparantly been making some changes
to the Nutella recipe.
#DontMessWithNutella #Nutella.'

—*Dailymail.com*, November 7, 2017, by Charlie Bayliss for mainonline.

Left Behind in Time

The small, battered tin trunk
wasn't much to look at
with its rusty hinges and dented sides

But inside
were one mother's treasured mementos
of the beloved son
who got left behind in time
having been killed
in 1917
during one of the bloodiest battles
of the First World War

The stained, small diary
a caricature sketched in the trenches
treasured photographs
and longed-for letters
were all perfectly preserved before being packed away
and forgotten
inside a dusty corner of the attic,
unseen
for almost 100 years

—Leda Reynolds for mainonline published in a *Daily Mail*, March 18, 2015, article
about letters between a mother and solider son who died during World War I.

Meg Eden

Found Poem in a Silver Spring Froyo Shop

Fruits are extremely important.
Fruits are high in
fruit, is linked:
disease,
cataracts,
great

Psalms of Anne

Oh! I'm becoming sensible!
I can't make you love me, Mother
noted, but where would you go?

I'll negotiate the stairs!
I'll practice being courageous!
Afterwards, I'll burn the pole!

I don't want to have lived in vain
like most people— all the women who go
about their work and are then forgotten.

I'm the kind of person you have to treat
with kid gloves! I'm carrying around a sweet
secret: in the future I'm going to devote
less time to sentimentality and more time to reality.

But we're stuck in this house like lepers.
—that doesn't suit Anne Frank in the least!

Paper has more patience than people.
Our own two feet are good enough for us.

Anyone who's so petty and pedantic at fifty-
four was born that way—I don't have to get
annoyed by their opinions,(but just this once,
I hope they'll be chosen for something good!)
There's not much you can do about inherited
traits; it's based on a mistake.

Gandhi is eating again to prove
the necessity of talking, but it probably
won't make a bit of difference. Later on,
neither I nor anyone else will be interested
in the musings of a thirteen year old school girl.

Memories mean more to me than dresses,
despite the mess and bother. I'm glad it hasn't deserted me.

—*The Diary of Anne Frank*

Propaganda Found Poem

Workers And Peasants, Join Hands and Advance!
We must have faith in the masses to defeat US aggressors.

Monsters of all kinds shall be destroyed when Mao
is the red sun in our hearts. Learning how to prepare

for war is the most spectacular of landscapes. We are found
on the most dangerous of summits, yet my heart is at ease—

Chairman Mao's instructions mean victory, and fighting hard
is our characteristic breaking of traditional ideas.

In the footsteps of the red army, our richest power is waging
war through the masses of the people—on earth the tiger has been
defeated.

Be a good child of the party, carrying the story of— the story—

Fight an abundant harvest! We will not accept a single apple.
New flowers bloom magnificently on their first attempt.

I am calling the stars to say, we have accomplished it!
Knowledge in pictures is the citizen's honorable duty.

Palace of youth, melody of youth—attack the book
of women! With you in charge, I regard the class struggle with
obedience.

   —Chinese propaganda posters

Sherri Bedingfield

A Plant Knows

1

Much to my surprise
the genetic difference
between plants and animals
is not as significant
as I once believed –
I question the parallels
between plant and human
biology, plant responses
to light and shadow
Light has properties shared
with other types of electrical
signals such as micro and radio
waves. Almost all plants
bend toward light.

2

We were confronted with
the remarkable discovery,
one can kill a cocklebur
leaf simply by touching it
for seconds each day. This
touch induced growth
inhibition is a general
phenomenon in plant
biology.

3

Defined plant memories,
procedural memories,
how to do things, these
memories depend on ability
to sense external stimulation—
if plants exhibit different
types of memory and have
a form of consciousness,
should they be considered
intelligent?

    —Daniel Chamovitz, "What a Plant Knows: A Field Guide to the Senses," *Scientific American*, 2012.

Sarah Webb

Hamilton County, C.S.A.

By 1860 had 489 people in 78 *families* from 15 states.
Vote in 1861 was *86-1 in favor of secession.*

60 farmers were organized as Hamilton County *Minutemen*
a unit of part-time soldiers. Others

joined Confederate regiments and *fought at Vicksburg Shiloh*
and other memorable battles. During the Civil War

travel was on horseback and hauling by *ox wagon.*
Homes were of logs split from *timber along creeks and rivers.*

About half an acre a day was farmed with homemade *wooden
tools.*
Corn and wheat were raised. *On burned-over ground*

each family grew its own tobacco
hanging the leaves inside the living room to dry.

Diet was mostly beef, cornbread and coffee substitutes.
Homes were lighted by wicks stuck into *tallow-filled eggshells.*

With few men on hand to brand and herd, *feuds rose* over thefts
and straying cattle.
In differences over war issues, 2 men *fled to Mexico* to join
Federals.

Later they returned, trying to recruit neighbors into a unit
disloyal to Texas
to welcome planned *Federal invasion.*

Further trouble came from many Confederate deserters
who took refuge *along the streams* and lived by theft and
violence.

—Historical Commission marker on Highway 281, north of Hamilton, Texas,
erected 1965.

Poem Found on a Visit to a High School Classroom

Teacher: *You're going to like this assignment, I promise.*
Student: *I don't like any assignment!*

Teacher, reading from literature book: *But the days passed and expectation gave way to resignation--the hopeless resignation of the old, sometimes miscalled apathy.*
Teacher: *What's apathy?*
Student: *You've got us. What's apathy?*

Teacher: *Let's do this now. We've got fifteen minutes.*
(Minute one)
Student: *Can I go to the bathroom?*
Teacher: *We need a paragraph, not a sentence.*
(Minute two)
Student: *I'm done!*
(Minute three)
Student: *What are you giving us this assignment for? We already have 200 points!*

Poster on the bulletin board: *Apathy is NOT an option!*
Poster by it: *We set high standards and we reach them.*
Student's shirt: *I'm not dumb--I just don't care!*

 —Classroom in Dibble High School, Dibble, Oklahoma. The story in literature book was "The Monkey's Paw" by W.W. Jacobs.

Pamela Guinan

The Wujek Coal Mine
13th - 16th December 1981

In Katowice, Poland, on December 16, 1981,
pacification turned deadly when police acting
against orders opened fire into an area occupied
by a group of striking miners, killing nine of the
striking miners assembled there.

The Beginning of a strike scenario was almost always
the same:
Information on the arrest of the leader
    of the company committee or its members
made the miners rebel,
    it gave them a feeling of injustice,
made them angry at the authorities
    and finally
aroused their willingness to demonstrate
    their opposition against the reality of
the situation.

In this first phase
they were also often accompanied by
    a feeling of
uncertainty and disorientation.

What followed were
often spontaneous preparations
from the hanging out of national flags
or information banners to the
    comprehensive
preparation of a work establishment
to defend itself against pacifying forces.
Most evidently
the authorities were more afraid of the dead
    witnesses of the tragedy at "Wujek"

than of the living.
A tribute to those
who passed away... too soon.

—Tomasz Nowara, *The Wujek Coal Mine 13th-16th December 1981. A tribute to those who passed away... too soon.* Translated by Magdalena Mariko-Kazaj. Katowice 2011.

Welfare on the Web—In Two Easy Columns

This
        website
is a
        quick and easy
way
        for people who live
in Connecticut
        to find out

        if they might be able
to get help with

ü Buying Food
ü Medical Benefits
ü Cash Assistance

This website
will take you
about 15 minutes
        to use.

We will ask you
        to tell us
        about
the people
in your home,
        the money
        you get from a job
        or other places,

your housing costs,
medical bills,
and expenses.
        What you tell us
        is private and secure.

When you are done,
        we will tell you

if you
and the people
in your home
may be

able

                  to get help
with:

buying food,
cash and medical
benefits.

    —Connecticut state government website

Sally Rhoades

Yet, Again, a Crackdown in Cambodia

Mu Sochua
OPINION
PHNOM PENH, CAMBODIA

1.

Kem Sokha, the leader of the opposition

      Cambodia National Rescue Party (C.N.R.P.),
was arrested during the early hours of Sept. 3,

        reportedly without a warrant and in violation
of his parliamentary immunity.

      Dozens of police officers surrounded his
home in Phnom Penh, while a group
        of armed men forced their way inside.

He has since been charged with treason—
and with conspiring with foreigners
to overthrow the Hun Sen government—
based on a 2013 speech in which

      he described wanting to bring peaceful,
        democratic change to Cambodia

     and receiving advise
        from American experts.

On Monday,
            during a session that the

C.N.R.P. boycotted,

            the National
            Assembly

            voted to allow the case
against Mr. Kem Sokha

            to proceed

            implicitly lifting his immunity.

Government-aligned media have named
            more purported participants
            in the spurious

            plot, intensifying the already
            palpable fear

            that anyone in our party, or anyone seen
as supporting it,
                        could be the government's
            next target.

            Several legislators
            who are senior
            members

            of the C.N.R.P.

have left the country
after being called

co-conspirators.

The
Independent media,
for their part,

are being wiped out.

The government
is invoking specious
tax bills or
contractual violations

to muzzle
outlets like

The Cambodia Daily,
Voice of America,
Radio Free Asia

and Voice of Democracy,

which have a
history of reporting

on controversial issues
like expropriation,
deforestation, and

government corruption.

3.

Last month
the local
office of the

National Democratic Institute,
an American pro-democracy

nonprofit
organization,

was abruptly
ordered to shut
down.

Other NGO's are being threatened
or bullied into silence. Over the past several
years, a spate of laws have been passed—

over objections
from the C.N.R.P.

and
civil society groups—restricting

the legitimate

activities of
political parties, trade unions
and NGO's and associations.

The assassination
of the outspoken political analyst

over a year ago has
      yet

          to be properly
          investigated.

      The ruling Cambodian People's party
         is cracking
           down

    ahead
    of the general election

       scheduled
      for next year because

    it fears for its prospects
    then.

4.

      In the last general
          election in 2013

the C.P.P. won 68 seats in the National Assembly—
down from 90—and the C.N.R.P. won 55, a record
for an opposition party. We also made impressive

    gains in local elections in June,
    winning control

    of 489 of the country's
    1646 communes—up from

the combined 40 communes
(out of 1,633) won in the 2012

    local elections by
     the two opposition

        parties that later
        merged

    to form
      the C.N.R.P.

These results may seem modest,
    but they are remarkable

    considering the C.P.P.'s
  lock on state resources and the
     increasingly repressive
       political climate
        in Cambodia.

And they prove that the C. N.R.P.
    appeals

       not only to the educated
       and the urban, but also

       to the rural poor,
       long the beneficiaries

       of the C.P.P. vast patronage
       networks.

If convicted of treason,
           Mr. Kem Sokha

faces up to 30 years in
prison.

Under recent revisions to the law
on political parties—

which ban parties from having leaders
with criminal records—

the C.N.R.P. would then be dissolved.
These legal changes have already forced

the C.N.R.P.'s former president,
Sam Rainsy, to resign

because he is the subject of
several (dubious) defamation
cases.

The government's game is transparent.

If Mr. Kem Sokha stays at the
helm of the C.N.R.P., the party

risks being dismantled. If he steps down,
more bogus charges will be brought against
our next leader—and then the next.

5.

Succumbing to the C.P.P. threat to disband us unless we
abandon our current leadership would be a grave political
error. We refuse to be complicit in this assault on democracy.

C.N.R.P. members and lawmakers have weathered various
onslaughts before, including arbitrary arrests and beatings

at the hands of the prime minister's own military bodyguards.

We have stood our ground out of faith in the power of the democratic process. Should our party be dissolved, the next general election would be a farce, and the next government,

a fraud.

—*The New York Times International Edition*, September 15, 2017.

Carol Dorf

Kick It

"Yes," she said, "He's kicking the world."
I paused, thinking of how to respond.
"Does he know he's kicking it?" I asked.
"That's the question," she replied.

—"Viola Frey: Who Makes Originals, Ever?" Interview by Richard Whittaker, works & conversations, Feb 2, 2001.

Take the Suggestion:

Look at the unknown!
This suggestion advises
you to do what you would do anyhow,
without any advice,
if you were seriously concerned
with your problem.
Are you hungry?
Have you a problem of any kind?

All the questions and suggestions
are natural, simple, obvious,
just plain common sense.
They suggest a certain conduct
which comes naturally
to any person
who is seriously concerned
with his problem.

But the person who behaves
the right way usually
does not care to express
his behavior in clear words.

—G. Polya, *How to Solve It*, 2nd ed., Princeton University Press, 1957.

I shake your hand

One day I hope you'll write.
How are your pains? Don't forget.

I'm going to start very early tomorrow
The shadows and cast shadows are removed;

I'll work again all day tomorrow
you can see how simple the idea is.

To take my revenge
The frame — will be white.

Solidity of the furniture --
unshakeable repose.

And that's all — nothing in this bedroom,
with its shutters closed.

The doors lilac, dressing table orange,
basin blue, window green.

The walls pale violet --
The floor — red tiles.

In short,
the colour has to do the job here,
to be suggestive *of rest* or *of sleep* in general
This time it's simply my bedroom

the direction the work is taking.
Because today I've gone back.

My dear

    —A reversal, from letter 705 that Vincent Van Gogh wrote to his brother, Theo, from Arles.

Lyman Grant

Usage Guide: Five Lesions

1. Silent Reading

No doubt,
Most

Of the prose
That finds

Its way
Into print

Is read
Aloud

By very
Few persons;

Some of it
Is

Perhaps
Never

So read
By anyone.

2. Easy-for-You-to-Say

American English
Has lately developed,
Largely under the influence
Of advertisers and packagers,
A construction deeply

At variance with the genius
Of the language.
We now have
Easy-to-read books
For children and
Ready-to-bake food
For their mothers.
This agglutination of ideas
Into complex phrases
Requiring hyphens
To make them into
Adjectives goes against
The normal articulation
Of thought.

3. Lousy Shoes

It is not worthwhile
To use *worthwhile*
Unless you split it
First to see whether
The *while* portion
Fits the context.

Time, in other words,
Must be involved in
The thing labeled
Worthwhile. This is why
We say *worthwhile*
Activities, such as sports

Hobbies, reading, etc.
But a sandwich cannot
Be worthwhile, or
A pair of shoes.

4. Upon Ishness

Everybody uses
Bookishness

As a derogatory
Term

But
Many of those
Who bandy
The word
About
Betray
The same fault
By a habitual use
Of *upon*
for *on,*
A substitution that
in modern prose
Does as much
To produce
A bookish effect
As any single
Word
Can
Do.

5. Able to Fly

We might
Call birds
And airline
Pilots volatile
But we don't.

—Wilson Follett, *Modern American Usage,* Hill & Wang, 1966.

Eighty-Seven Billion
(A poem liberated from George W. Bush's address to the nation 9/7/03)

> I have asked for this time
> in a series of raids and actions

leaders have been captured and killed
this undertaking is difficult and costly
a grave setback for international terrorism

> I have asked for this time
> our enemies understand this

there is more at work than blind rage
America has done this kind of work before
we will do what is necessary

> I have asked for this time
> we are sending a clear message

I have expressed confidence
we will keep our word
miseries and humiliation inflicted

> I have asked for this time
> there will be no going back

the heaviest burdens in our war
after oppression and mismanagement
are not caused by the use of strength

> I have asked for this time
> thank you and good night

John Milkereit

Eating Right Because

most diets are about losing.
The Abs Diet is about gaining.
The Abs Diet is based on the
simple notion that your body
is a living, breathing,
calorie-burning machine,
and that by keeping
your body's fat furnace
constantly stoked with lots
and lots of the right foods—
and this is important—
at the right time, you can
teach it to start burning off
your belly in no time. In fact,
this diet can help you burn
up to 12 pounds of fat—
from your belly first—
in 2 weeks or less.
And just look at
what you'll
gain in
return.

—David Zinczenko, *The Abs Diet*. Rodale Inc., 2004.

Best Bag Ever!

These bags have been loaded,
unloaded, stuffed,
crammed, tossed,
thrown and smooshed—
only to come
home again and
again
in one piece.

—L.L. Bean Catalogue, 2017.

Why Get An Agent?

"I don't care if I'm edited by Genghis Khan,"
I cried, "just pick one person for me to work
with and let me get on with it!"
No such luck. My relationship
with the publishing company rapidly
started going down the tubes.
I began embracing Buddhism,
chanting the mantra "Better published
than not published," in an effort
to see the silver lining
in the darkening cloud
hovering over

—Peter Rubie, *The Everything Get Published Book,* Adams Media Corporation, 2000.

Kathy Douglas

Moods and Madness

You're not
at all
like springs,
for all the winters;
you are tedious
beyond belief:
no reassurance is ever enough.
But these experiences carry
thought faster
and I cannot imagine
medicine and love
broken.
I have crawled
on my hands,
worn death
as close as
my mind,
loved
faster than
most, finding
new corners
I cannot
imagine
becoming
jaded to.

—Kay Redfield Jamison, *An Unquiet Mind: A Memoir of Moods and Madness*,
Random House, 1996.

The Blue of Desire

Blue is
the color
of desire, the color
of where you are
Often it is
desire as a problem
rather than
desire that fills
Blue is
distance without
your longing
for that blue
At its edges,
the poet says,
something of this longs
to be relocated
Never go for the way
of perspective,
you never arrive.
Desire fills
the distance between
blue sky
and blue at the horizon
on its own terms

—Rebecca Solnit, *A Field Guide to Getting Lost*, Penguin Books, 2005.

I Don't Like Giving Up Either

In the spirit of transparency,
I know every fine grain
of said shit, and then some

I'm not sorry about what I said
last night—*This is not my home*

With the world the way it is,
you're going to find yourself in a place
that can't be undone—

There's a vast ocean of shit
you don't know shit about—
And I'm sorry I didn't say it sooner.

But we can block the view—
we do it together. Nightmares end.
The storm hit and we found each other.
This is the real world,
and maybe you don't have to die

You brought your people to safety
because all life is precious.

Lead them to the fence,
don't be long.

—"Conquer." AMC. The Walking Dead, Season 5, 29 March 2015.

Geraldine Zetzel

Don't Open the Door

Move quickly: the odds
of survival are highest
if you get out
in the first 60 seconds.
If there are children present
unfasten them from the back seat
push them out the window
oldest ones first.

In a submersion study
three passengers were able to exit
with a child mannequin
in just 53 seconds.

Electric car windows will
likely continue to work
after impact with water. Still,
keep a small glass-breaking
tool on your key-ring or hanging
from the rearview mirror,
just in case.

—"How To Escape from a Car in Water," *The New York Times*, April 16, 2017.

David K. Leff

Big Bill's Strings
(with Big Bill Broonzy)

*Hey hey I made a date with an angel. Come home early long tall
mamma, I can't be satisfied worrying you off my mind with
whiskey and good time blues, bricks on my pillow.*

*I believe I'll go back home. I'm gonna move to the outskirts of
town, going back to Arkansas with too many drivers holding a
key to the highway having too too train blues.*

*It's a low down dirty shame, but I want my hand
on it, that house rent stomp and flat foot Susie with her
flat yes yes. Horny frog, you've got to hit the right lick.*

    —Big Bill Broonzy song titles

Lightnin' Strikes
(with Lightning Hopkins)

Woke up this morning, trouble in mind, bad luck and trouble,
lonesome dog. Give back that wig bald headed woman, tell me
ain't it lonesome.

Come on baby, love like a hydrant. Take me back money taker,
shake yourself. Beans, beans, beans: I'll meet
you at the chicken shack.

Watch my fingers, I once was a gambler. So bottle up
and go, get off my toe, the foot race is on. In the evening the sun
is going down.

    —Lightnin' Hopkins song titles

Slim's Keys
(with Memphis Slim)

Nobody loves me but me, myself and I so lend me your love beer drinking woman, maybe I'll lend you a dime. We're two of a kind, angel child.

Every day I have the blues—empty room blues, blues at midnight, the jive blues, whiskey and gin blues and grinder man blues. You got to help me some.

You didn't mean me no good messin' around, but you gonna worry too much. I see my great mistake so throw this poor dog a bone.

Kilroy has been here, so I believe I'll settle down, rockin' the house, diggin' my potatoes, Harlem bound in my last pair of shoes blues.

    —Memphis Slim song titles

Chesley Park

Look In Their Eyes, Ma

My mother always had the radio on when I came
down into the kitchen in the morning.

I guess when I was in my teens, she was probably,
I don't know, ten years younger than me.

She was but a girl, you know, and she liked
that rock 'n' roll music.

Every morning we'd be down there,
she'd have the local Top 40 station on.

Throughout most of my young life,
it was the music that gave me a sense

of just living and having fun, and that life
could be more than what I saw

around me, you know, and should be more
if you could make it so.

    —Marc Dolan, *Bruce Springsteen and the Promise of Rock 'n' Roll,* W.W. Norton,
2012.

The New Enlightenment

Every time
you feel hunger
or taste ambition
Every time
your body tingles with lust
or your heart yearns
for recognition
Every time
you shake with anger
or tremble in fear
that's the animal in you
striving for life

We fall into the world
caught between two
necessities –
compelled to live
born to die –
and reconciling them
has forever been
one of our most
challenging puzzles
The pieces
just don't
fit together

 —Roy Scranton, *Learning to Die in the Anthropocene*, City Lights
Books, 2015.

Forked and Playful as Lightning

The actual word electricity came into mind
no doubt because the word lightning
was already there on the page

It didn't bother me that I couldn't think
of many crested serpents
a cobra perhaps with those bits

at the side of its head quivering or perhaps
he meant the arched neck crested like a wave
as the serpent gets set to strike

Possibly there was a crested serpent
somewhere in Shakespeare
and Hazlitt was making a subtle reference

or Shakespeare might have had a crested servant
and Hazlitt was remembering a sequence
of sounds rather than specific meaning

What mattered was the balance
between two pictures
the first of things happening

very quickly at random
and the second a pause a poise
matched by two contrary movements

of the sentence prancing up to the comma
and then turning deliberate,
after it the double compliment

—Clive James, *Cultural Amnesia*, W.W. Norton 2007.

All That Still Lies Beneath the Surface

But as with much that is ugly,
there is value in the products,
particularly when
the aesthetic flaws
are the only ones.
Berries can be too small,
cucumbers crooked,
bananas fat –
and all can be bruised
or blemished –
without harming their taste
or health benefits.
A truly ugly tomato
can still be perfect
for a juice or a sauce.

    —*The Economist*, January 13-19, 2018.

Thomasina Levy

Gasconading Bluster

... best not make any more threats
to the United States

they will be met with
FIRE and FURY
like the world
has never seen.

He has been very threatening
beyond a normal state
And as I said before,
They will be met with
FIRE,
FURY,
and frankly
POWER

The like of which
this world
Has NEVER seen before.

Thank you...

     —*The New York Times*, August 9, 2017.

Sharon R. Chace

United Airlines Flight Attendant
to a Young Family
June 18, 2011

"Take it all in.
Take pictures:
The big trees,
Their smells.
Be careful with
The animals.
Stay together.
Don't get lost."

—This was previously published in *Cape Ann and Beyond the Cut Bridge Culling and Cart-wheeling*.

Imperative

A boy about eight years old to his parents
who were taking pictures from the top of
Sulphur Mountain in Banff National Park,
Canada

"Never delete the rainbow.
Never delete the rainbow."

Ann Marie Cologna

Keep Going

If you're going through hell—keep going.

For continuous effort—not strength or intelligence
is key to unlocking our potential.

You'll make all kinds of mistakes;
 but as long as you are generous,
true and fierce,
you cannot hurt the world—
or even seriously distress her.

This is no time for ease or comfort.
It's time to dare and endure.

Can people tax themselves into prosperity?

Can a man stand on a bucket
and lift himself up by the handle?

There is only one thing worse
than fighting with allies—
that's fighting without them.

You have enemies—good!
Then you have stood for something—
sometime in your life.

Tact is the ability to tell someone to go to hell
in such a way they look forward to the trip,
and success is the ability to go
from one failure to another with enthusiasm.

So if you are going through hell—keep going.

—The sayings of Winston Churchill

Eddie Morales

The Burning of Bishop Nicholas Ridley (1555)

These were the conditions
in which the future Bishop
passed the years of his childhood.

At Unthank he was protected by
no King
or justice,
but owed his life to the courage
and ruthlessness of his family. . .
Every night, they drove their cattle
within the walls of their strong stone houses
to protect them from the thieves;
But often worse dangers were at hand.

A horseman would bring news that
the Scottish raiders had crossed the border,
and Nicholas saw his kinsmen put on their
jacks and seize their spears as they prepared
to defend their homes. . .

but one would hardly have expected the
conditions in the Marches to encourage
a religious and pious frame of mind,
still, less to produce distinguished churchmen.

Churchmen, to be later burned at the stake
for their most pious beliefs.

—Jasper Godwin Ridley, *Nicholas Ridley, A Biography*, Longmans Green, 1957.

Mindfulness

The cultivation of mindfulness
may just be the hardest
work in all the world.
When it comes to mindfulness,
each of us brings
our own genius
to adventures of this kind.

Moreover,
we cannot help but make
use of and build
on everything that has
come before in our lives,

even if much of it was—
and perhaps still is—
painful.

—Jon Kabat-Zinn, *Mindfulness for Beginners*, Sounds True, 2016.

The Contributors

The Editor

Jonas Zdanys, a bilingual poet and translator, is the author of forty-eight other books. Forty-four of those are collections of his own poetry, written in English or in Lithuanian, and volumes of his translations into English of Lithuanian poetry and fiction. He has received a number of prizes, book awards, writing and travel grants, and public recognitions for his own poetry and for his translations. He has taught at the State University of New York and at Yale University, where he also held a number of administrative positions. He served for more than a decade as the state of Connecticut's Chief Academic Officer and is currently Professor of English and Poet in Residence at Sacred Heart University, where he teaches creative writing and modern poetry seminars and directs the program in creative writing. More at jonaszdanys.org

The Poets

Laura Altshul's *Searching for the Northern Lights* was published in 2015 and *Bodies Passing* in 2017. Her poems have appeared in *Connecticut River Review, The Perch, Forgotten Women*, and *Serving House Journal*. She was awarded 1st place in the Al Savard Memorial Contest, New York Poetry Forum, Tennessee Poetry Society and has given readings throughout Connecticut and at Yale. She was featured on Public TV's *Speaking of Poetry Episode 36*.

Joseph Bathanti is former Poet Laureate of North Carolina (2012-14) and recipient of the 2016 North Carolina Award for Literature. He is the author of ten books of poetry, including *Communion Partners*; *Anson County*; *The Feast of All Saints*; *This Metal*, nominated for the National Book Award, and winner of the Oscar Arnold Young Award; *Land of Amnesia*; *Restoring Sacred Art*, winner of the 2010 Roanoke Chowan Prize, awarded annually by the North Carolina Literary and Historical Association for best book of poetry in a given year; *Sonnets of the Cross*; *Concertina*, winner of the 2014 Roanoke Chowan Prize; and *The 13th Sunday after Pentecost*, released by LSU Press in 2016. His novel, *East Liberty*, won the 2001 Carolina Novel Award. His novel, *Coventry*, won the 2006 Novello Literary Award. His book of stories, *The High Heart*, won the 2006 Spokane Prize. *They Changed the State: The*

Legacy of North Carolina's Visiting Artists, 1971-1995 was published in early 2007. His recent book of personal essays, *Half of What I Say Is Meaningless*, winner of the Will D. Campbell Award for Creative Nonfiction, is from Mercer University Press. A new novel, *The Life of the World to Come*, was released from University of South Carolina Press in 2014. He is Professor of Creative Writing at Appalachian State University in Boone, North Carolina, and the University's Watauga Residential College Writer-in-Residence.

Sherri (Sheryll) Bedingfield's poetry has appeared in several anthologies and small press publications including *Caduceus, Journal of Poetry Therapy* and *Connecticut River Review*. She has presented her poetry at Connecticut venues including West Hartford Art League, Word Forge Poetry Series in Hartford, Windsor Art Center, Wintonbury Poetry Series, Hartford Public Library, and Yale Book Store. Her poems have been performed by East Haddam Stage Company in Plays with Poetry. She acted the roles of two minor poets from the nineteenth century in a staged performance at the Hill-Stead Museum, called The Haunted Shelves of Hill-Stead. Sherri portrayed the ghost of Edna St. Vincent Millay in her own skit at the Buttonwood Tree in Middletown, Connecticut. One of her poems was selected by West Hartford, Connecticut, town poet laureates, past and present, as a finalist for the Poetry in the Parks Projects and is displayed at Westmoor Park in West Hartford over the summer season. She also did the art work that frames the poem. In July 2015, Sherri read her poetry in Dingle, Ireland. A book of her poems, *Transitions and Transformations*, was published in September 2010 by Antrim House. She did the artwork on its cover. In 2016 her book *The Clattering, Voices from Old Forfarshire, Scotland* was published. Sherri works as a psychotherapist and a family therapist.

Chantel Langlinais Carlson is an Instructor of English at Texas Christian University, where she teaches modern drama and poetry, creative writing, film, gender studies, and composition. She is both a playwright and a poet. Her one-act play, *The Exhibit*, was published by Next Stage Press. Her poetry is forthcoming in The Louisiana Review and *The Southern Poetry Anthology, Volume VIII: Texas* and has appeared in *Writing Texas*, *Truck*, *The Louisiana Review*, damselfly press, and *The Southwestern Review*. Her poetry chapbook, *Turning 25*, was published by Nous-zot Press. Her work has also been published in the *Interdisciplinary Humanities Journal* and the *Louisiana English*

Journal. She received both her M.A. and Ph.D. from the University of Louisiana at Lafayette.

Sharon R. Chace describes herself as an older but intellectually lively artist and writer. In 1966 she received a B.A. degree from Albion College in Albion, Michigan, with a major in art and minors in English and religion. In 1998 she received a Master of Theological Studies degree (M.T.S.) with a Biblical concentration from Weston Jesuit School of Theology, where she was a Protestant wildcard. Jesuits helped her find her voice in poetry and prose: during a course on Ignatian spirituality, her writing career became clear. She is now the Poet Laureate of Rockport, Massachusetts. More can be found at sharonchace.com.

Sandra Chaff is an attorney and archivist who lives in Philadelphia. Her work has appeared in *Poet Lore, Six,* and the 2017 *Moonstone Featured Poets Anthology,* among other publications. She is a founding member of the long-running poetry collective 34th Street Poets, who have performed their poetry in and around Philadelphia, including as part of the 2014 Philadelphia Fringe Festival.

Vicki Collins teaches English at the University of South Carolina, Aiken. Her work has appeared in *Kakalak, MoonShine Review, Windhover, Barbaric Yawp, The Teacher's Voice, The Southern Poetry Anthology: North Carolina, The South Carolina Encyclopedia Guide to South Carolina Writers,* and several Old Mountain Press anthologies. Her book, *The Silent Appalachian: Wordless Mountaineers in Fiction, Film, and Television,* was published in 2017 by McFarland.

Ann Marie Cologna is a member of the Meriden Poetry Society in Connecticut. Her first book of poetry, *Poetry for the Rest of Us,* was published in November 2017. It is a collection of poems, which she calls the blood-letting of emotion, written from 1979 to 2017.

t. l. (Terri Lynn) Cummings is a Frequent Contributor to *Songs of Eretz Poetry Review.* Her poems appear in *Red River Review, Eclectica, Illya's Honey, Dragon Poet Review,* and elsewhere. Her work is found in several anthologies, including *Malpais Review* and *Woody Guthrie Poems: Ain't Gonna Be Treated This Way.* Terri is a Mark Allen Everett Poet at the University of Oklahoma, and hosts Oklahoma Voices: First Sunday Poetry Series in Oklahoma City. In addition, she presents her work in numerous symposia and workshops. Village Books Press published her first poetry book, *Tales to the Wind* (2016), and chapbook *An Element Apart* (2017). She studied at Creative Writing Institute and holds a B.S. in Sociology/Anthropology from Oklahoma State University. Terri continues to explore cultural humanity while she and her husband travel the world.

William Virgil Davis's most recent book of poetry is *Dismantlements of Silence: Poems Selected and New* (2015). He has published five other books of poetry: *The Bones Poems; Landscape and Journey*, which won the New Criterion Poetry Prize and the Helen C. Smith Memorial Award for Poetry; *Winter Light; The Dark Hours*, which won the Calliope Press Chapbook Prize; and *One Way to Reconstruct the Scene*, which won the Yale Series of Younger Poets Prize. His poems have appeared in most of the major periodicals, here and abroad, including *Agenda, The Atlantic Monthly, The Gettysburg Review, The Georgia Review, The Harvard Review, The Hopkins Review, The Hudson Review The Nation, The Malahat Review, The New Criterion, PN Review, Poetry, The Sewanee Review, Southwest Review, The Southern Review*, and *TriQuarterly*, among many others.

J.S. Dennis is a pen name used by a poet, translator, editor, teacher, and reviewer.

Joanie DiMartino has work published in many literary journals and anthologies, including *Modern Haiku, Alimentum, Calyx*, and *Circe's Lament: An Anthology of Wild Women*. She is a past winner of the Betty Gabehart Award for Poetry. DiMartino is the author of two collections of poetry, *Licking the Spoon* and *Strange Girls*, and is completing her third manuscript, "Wood to Skin," about the 19th-century whaling industry, for which she was a 38th Voyager on the Charles W. Morgan. Visit her website at www.joaniedimartino.com.

Carol Dorf has two chapbooks available, *Some Years Ask* (Moria Press) and *Theory Headed Dragon* (Finishing Line Press.) Her poetry appears in *The Mom Egg, Sin Fronteras, E-ratio, Great Weather For Media, About Place, Glint, Slipstream, Surreal Poetics, About Place, The Journal of Humanistic Mathematics, Scientific American*, and *Maintenant*. She is poetry editor of *Talking Writing* and teaches math at Berkeley High School.

Kathy Douglas is a Connecticut-based poet who is currently writing a coffee table book of what she calls "coffee table poems" composed weekly on her living room coffee table. She recently completed a book of blackout poems titled *On The Ward of Omens* based on Mary Daly's *Beyond God the Father: Toward A Philosophy of Women's Liberation.* Her work has been published online and in print in *Right Hand Pointing, After the Pause, Unlost Journal, Calyx, Nocturna, The Café Review, Drunken Boat, Praxilla, shufpoetry*, and *Poetry WTF?!* and she has work forthcoming in *Writers Resist.* More can be found at medium.com/@kathrynd and on Twitter @kathydouglas. She holds an MFA in Poetry from Bennington College, an MFA in Museum Studies from Syracuse University, and a BA in Studio Art from the State University of New York, Potsdam. She is a National Poetry Month Scout Laureate, PoMoSco, Found Poetry Review 2015 National Poetry Month Project, and a proud graduate of the UC Irvine MOOC, Society, Science, Survival: Lessons From AMC's 'The Walking Dead. She is Senior Associate Director of Career Development at Yale School of Forestry & Environmental Studies.

Meg Eden's work is published or forthcoming in magazines including *Prairie Schooner, Poetry Northwest, Poet Lore, RHINO*, and *CV2*. She teaches creative writing at the University of Maryland. She has five poetry chapbooks, and her novel *Post-High School Reality Quest* is published with California Coldblood, an imprint of Rare Bird Books. More at www.megedenbooks.com or on Twitter @ConfusedNarwhal.

Gregory Ellis received his B.A. from Amherst College in 1972, a J.D. from UCLA School of Law in 1985, and an MFA in Writing from Vermont College of Fine Arts in 1994. While at Amherst, he majored in music and studied writing with Tillie Olsen when she was writer-in-residence. Beginning in the early 1970's, he has sung and played guitar in nightclubs throughout the country. In 2010, he published his first novel, *Ride the Buffalo's Back*. He lives with his family in the Los Angeles area where he practices appellate law, continues to perform in local clubs, and is at work on his second novel, *Jesus' Other Brother*.

James Finnegan's poems have appeared in *Ploughshares, Poetry Northwest, The Southern Review, The Virginia Quarterly Review*, as well as in the anthology *Good Poems: American Places* edited by Garrison Keillor. With Dennis Barone he edited *Visiting Wallace:*

Poems Inspired by the Life and Work of Wallace Stevens. He is the president of the Friends & Enemies of Wallace Stevens (stevenspoetry.org). His aphoristic *ars poetica* can be found at the blog ursprache, http://ursprache.blogspot.com.

Maria Mazziotti Gillan is the author of twenty-two books. Her newest poetry collection is *What Blooms in Winter* (NYQ 2016). She received the American Book Award for *All That Lies Between Us* (Guernica Editions). Ms. Gillan is the Founder and Executive Director of the Poetry Center at Passaic County Community College in Paterson, New Jersey, and editor of the *Paterson Literary Review*. She is also Director of the Creative Writing Program and Professor of Poetry at Binghamton University-SUNY.

Jennifer Glick lives in Wethersfield, Connecticut. A nurse/social worker and Vietnam veteran, she is newly retired and able to dedicate more time to writing poetry and creating collages. Often she can be found on her zafu, meditating on letting go of the desire to be published.

Patricia Goodrich is both a poet and visual artist. Featured at writers' conferences in Slovenia, Lithuania, Romania, Russia, and the USA, she has received Pennsylvania Fellowships in Poetry and Creative Nonfiction and was a Pew Foundation finalist in Creative Nonfiction. Her poetry collections include *Woman With a Wandering Eye, How the Moose Got To Be, Verda's House, Red Mud*, and *Stone Hunting in Transylvania*, companion editions in English and in Romanian translation. More at patriciagoodrich.com

Lyman Grant, recently retired, worked at Austin Community College for almost 40 years as a professor and administrator. He has edited two textbooks and four anthologies, and he has published five volumes of poems, most recently *Old Men on Tuesday Mornings* (Alamo Bay Press).

Pamela Guinan began writing poetry more or less seriously in the nineteen-nineties. Her first work of that era was a stream of consciousness poem, "Big Soft-Hards." Her work is published in the Faxon Poets chapbook, *Perspectives*. She is a member of the Connecticut Poetry Society, where she has served as president of the Middletown Chapter since 2011. She earned a Bachelor of General Studies from the University of Connecticut (2016).

Vernita Hall won the Marsh Hawk Press Robert Creeley Prize for her first full-length poetry volume *Where William Walked* (as yet unpublished, judge Meena Alexander). *The Hitchhiking Robot Learns About Philadelphians* won the Moonstone Chapbook Contest (judge Afaa Michael Weaver). She placed second in American Literary Review's Creative Nonfiction Contest, and second runner-up for the Los Angeles Review Nonfiction Award. Poetry and essays appear in numerous journals, including *Atlanta Review, Philadelphia Stories, Referential, Mezzo Cammin, Canary, African American Review*; and nine anthologies, including *Forgotten Women* (Grayson Books), *Not Our President* (Third World Press), and *Dear America: Reflections on Race* (Geeky Press). An MFA in Creative Writing graduate from Rosemont College, she serves on the poetry review board of Philadelphia Stories.

Michelle Hartman's latest book is *The Lost Journal of My Second Trip to Purgatory*, from Old Seventy Creek Press. It is the first poetic look at child abuse and its effects on adult life, and the first book of its kind from a recognized publisher. Along with her poetry books, *Irony and Irreverence* and *Disenchanted and Disgruntled*, from Lamar University Press, *Lost Journal* is available on Amazon. She is the editor of *Red River Review*. Hartman holds a B.S. in Political Science, Pre-Law, from Texas Wesleyan University and a Paralegal certificate from Tarrant County College. She also has a chapbook out from El Grito Del Lobo Press, *There are no Doors*.

Van Hartmann is Professor of English at Manhattanville College. He received his B.A. in History from Stanford University and his Ph.D. in English from the University of North Carolina. His poetry has appeared in numerous journals. He has published two books of poetry, *Shiva Dancing*, Texture Press, 2007, and *Riptide*, Texture Press, 2016, and a chapbook, *Between What Is and What Is Not*, The Last Automat Press, 2010. He lives in Norwalk, Connecticut, with his wife and fellow poet, Laurel Peterson. He can be contacted at Van.Hartmann@mville.edu or at van.hartmann@gmail.com.

A.C. Jerroll is a pen name sometimes used by a publishing poet, fiction writer, reviewer, and editor.

Jennifer Kidney is an adjunct assistant professor for the College of Professional and Continuing Studies at the University of Oklahoma. She is the author of six books of poetry: *Field Encounters* (Full Count Press, 1981), *Endangered Species* (Renegade/Point Riders Press, 1984), *Animal Magnetism* (Wowapi, 1985), *Women Who Sleep with the Dogs* (Village Books Press, 2004), *Life List* (Village Books Press, 2007), and *Road Work Ahead* (Village Books Press, 2012).

Susan King gave her career to teaching literature, reading, and art at Howard College in Big Spring, Texas. She reads much, writes some, and continues to teach an occasional class in art history or literature.

Professional performance artist and publisher Janet Kuypers (janetkuypers.com) edits two literary magazines (*cc&d*, and *Down in the Dirt*) while running Scars Publications (http://scars.tv). A multiple Pushcart Prize nominee and highlighted on radio and national and local television, she has 90+ books published (poetry, prose, novels, art), sung in 3 bands with shows around the U.S., and her CD releases (40+) appear at iTunes & other online vendors. She also hosted "the Café Gallery" Chicago poetry open mike (http://scars.tv/thecafe) from 2010 - 2015, with weekly poetry videos and podcasts. She currently performs 12-25 poetry readings/shows per year. Her most recent books are "(pheromemes) 2015-2017 poems" http://scars.tv/pheromemes/pheromemes2015-2017poems.htm; "(pheromemes) 2015-2017 show poems" http://scars.tv/pheromemes/pheromemes2015-2017show-poems.htm

David K. Leff is an essayist, Pushcart nominated poet, and former Deputy Commissioner of the Connecticut Department of Environmental Protection. His work focuses on the surprisingly intimate relationship of people to their built and natural environments. His nonfiction book *The Last Undiscovered Place* (University of Virginia Press, 2004) was a Connecticut Book Award finalist. He is the author of four other nonfiction books, *Deep Travel* (University of Iowa Press, 2009), *Hidden in Plain Sight* (Wesleyan University Press, 2012), *Maple Sugaring: Keeping it Real in New England* (Wesleyan University Press, 2015), and *Canoeing Maine's Legendary Allagash: Thoreau, Love, and Survival of the Wild* (Homebound Publications, 2016). His poetry collections are *The Price of Water* (Antrim House, 2008), *Depth of Field* (Antrim House, 2010), and *Tinker's Damn* (Homebound Publications, 2013). His novel in verse, *Finding the Last Hungry Heart* (Homebound Publications, 2014), is about the confluence of the present and the 1960s. His work has appeared in the

Hartford Courant, The Wayfarer, Appalachia, Yankee, Connecticut Woodlands, Connecticut Coastal, Canoe & Kayak, The Encyclopedia of New England, and elsewhere. His writing is available at www.davidkleff.com

Connecticut State Troubadour (2005/2006), Thomasina Levy, is an award winning, internationally recognized mountain dulcimer player, singer, poet, and song writer. With a Master of Science degree in Education, she uses music and art to help students of all ages discover their own creative spirits throughout the United States. She is a Teaching Artist with the Connecticut Office of the Arts, helping fellow artists, educators, schools and museums incorporate music, poetry and visual art into their programs. Her music has been aired in over twenty countries across the globe, and she has recordings and instructional books for both children and adults. Her most recent recording project, "Out of Many We Are One," received the 2011 NAMA Award for "Best Song/Single of the Year." Her poem, "Evensong," was recently published on the Connecticut Poetry Society's website. For more information, please see www.dulcimersong

Nathan Lewis is a painter whose work has been exhibited nationally and internationally. His work is also in private collections in New York, Connecticut, Massachusetts, California, Russia, Germany, and India. Recent exhibitions include "Dreams, Discord and Desire: Nathan Lewis" at Oglethorpe University Museum of Art in Atlanta, "Marking Time—New Explorations in drawing," at the Dishman Museum in Texas, and "Speak to Me: the Connecticut Biennial" at the Mattatuck Museum of Art. He has consistently participated in solo and group exhibitions at galleries, museums, and universities throughout the United States. His paintings have been on the cover of numerous books and journals, and his work was included in films shown at the Cannes and Sundance Film festivals. He serves presently as Associate Professor of Art at Sacred Heart University.

Patricia Martin is an author, poet, performer/actor, and freelance writer/communications professional. She has been featured at numerous venues, including The Museum of the Imagination, The Howland Cultural Center, The Dissident Arts Festival, The Woodstock Fringe, The Byrdcliff Theatre, and The National Beat Poetry Festival's "Kerouac Café," among others. Martin has been heard on The Woodstock RoundTable/WDST and Women of Note/WKZE, is a monthly guest on "She's Raising the Bar" radio show, and has been published in *Chronogram, The County and Abroad, Art Times, Chatham Magazine, WaterWrites*, and other periodicals. A member of the Author's Guild, Martin is the author of one humor book, five nonfiction books, a spoken word & music CD with composer/producer Gus Mancini. She founded the monthly poetry/spoken word series SpeakEasy in March 2017. Her books include *Worms of Wisdom* (Great Quotations); *Words from Great Women* (Great Quotations); *Ancient Echoes: Native American Words of Wisdom* (Great Quotations); *Modern Woman: A Stress-Relief Manual* (Great Quotations); *Growing Up in Toyland: Our All-Time, Best-Loved Toys* (Great Quotations); and *The Right Side of Forty: Celebrating Timeless Women* (Conari Press, now an imprint of Red Wheel/Weiser).

John Milkereit is a rotating equipment engineer working at an engineering contracting firm in Houston. His poems have appeared in various literary journals such as *Texas Poetry Calendar* and *San Pedro River Review*. His chapbooks are *Home & Away* and *Paying Admissions* (Pudding House Press, 2010). He recently completed a low-residency M.F.A. program in Creative Writing at the Rainier Writing Workshop in Tacoma, Washington. His collection of poems, *A Rotating Equipment Engineer is Never Finished*, was published March 2015 (Ink Brush Press).

Eddie Morales has been writing poetry for over twenty years and has published eleven books of poetry. He currently resides in Wallingford, Connecticut. For more information, please visit his website www.poeticon.com

Tom Nicotera has been a factory worker, street performer, mime, water/sewer repairman, copy editor, library cataloger, and teacher, while keeping poetry as the one constant in his life. In Washington, D.C., he was co-producer of a jazz/poetry day at the Washington Monument and ran the Takoma Cafe Poetry Series in Maryland. In Connecticut, he edited *Charter Oak Poets II*, a collection of works from Hartford area writers, and served on the organizing committee for the 2001 Connecticut Poetry Festival at Middlesex Community College. He has published poems in numerous small press publications, and his poems have been performed by the East Haddam Stage Co. in Connecticut. Tom is currently co-host of Bloomfield (Connecticut) Library's Wintonbury Poetry Series and a member of a performance poetry trio called "Not Just Any Tom, Vic and Terri." His poetry book, *What Better Place To Be Than Here?* was published by Foothills Publishing in 2015.

Vivian Finley Nida is a Teacher/Consultant with the Oklahoma Writing Project, affiliated with the University of Oklahoma. Her work has appeared in the *Oklahoma Writing Project Centennial Anthology, Oklahoma English Journal, Westview: Journal of Western Oklahoma, Illya's Honey, Dragon Poet Review, River Poets Journal "Windows" edition, Westview: Journal of Western Oklahoma, Songs of Eretz Poetry Review*, and the 2017 *Woody Guthrie Poetry Anthology*. Mrs. Nida holds a B.A. in English and an M.S. in Secondary Education from Oklahoma State University and is a retired teacher of English, Creative Writing, and Advanced Composition. She lives in Oklahoma City.

Kansas City, Missouri-born, Marian O'Brien Paul lived in Turkey, a military wife (1972-75). A Fulbright lecturer (1987-88), she taught at Çukurova University, Adana, Turkey. Six months in a cottage near Rossport, County Mayo, Ireland (2002), helped her complete her dissertation (PhD 2003). Retired from teaching at Omaha, Nebraska's Metropolitan Community College (2006), she's now in Chicago. Her poems appear in *Skylight 47 Poetry*, Galway, Ireland, Sept 2016; *Englyn - Journal of Four Line Poetry*, April 2016; *Pushing the Envelope: Epistolary Poems*, ed. Jonas Zdanys, Lamar University Press, 2015; *Eastlit*, March 2015; *Yale Journal of Humanities in Medicine*, July 2014. An upcoming anthology by A Room of Her Own Foundation has accepted an excerpt from her longer poem in *Virginia Woolf and the Arts: Selected Papers from the Sixth Annual Conference on Virginia Woolf, 1997*. Her prose story "Ladybug, Ladybug, Fly Away Home" appeared in *the Liguorian Magazine*, October 2015.

Gay Paluch has been writing poetry for many years and is presently a member of the Monson Poets and Florence Poets Society, both located in Western Massachusetts. Her collection of nature poems, *Just This Morning*, was published in 2012. She has been published in *Silkworm, Freshwater, Common Ground Review*, and American *Chestnut Society Journal*.

Chesley Park is a writer and former government official who spends time in Maine.

Laurel S. Peterson is Professor of English at Norwalk Community College. Her poetry has been published in many small literary journals. She has two poetry chapbooks: *That's the Way the Music Sounds*, (Finishing Line Press, 2009) and *Talking to the Mirror* (The Last Automat Press, 2010). She also co-edited a collection of essays on women's justice titled *(Re)Interpretations: The Shapes of Justice in Women's Experience* (2009). Her mystery novel, *Shadow Notes*, was released by Barking Rain Press (2016), and the second in the series will be out in 2018. Her full-length poetry collection, *Do You Expect Your Art to Answer You?*, was published by Futurecycle Press in 2017. She is the current poet laureate of Norwalk, Connecticut.

Amie E. Reilly is an adjunct instructor in the Department of English at Sacred Heart University in Connecticut, where she lives with her husband and ten-year-old son. Her most recent work can be found at *Fiction Advocate, The New Engagement, The Evansville Review*, and *Entropy*. She also blogs at https://theshapeofme.blog/

Sally Rhoades, a former Capital reporter in Albany, N.Y., began writing poetry in the late 1980's. She has published in *Elegant Rage*, a poetic tribute honoring the centennial of Woody Guthrie, the *Highwatermark Salo[o]n* performance series by Stockpot flats, *Up the River by Albany Poets*, and *Peerglass*, an anthology of Hudson Valley peer groups. She was featured on the podcast, Poetry Spoken Here, by Charlie Rossiter that debuted on September 15, 2017. She is also a performance artist and playwright. She lives in Albany, N. Y. with her husband Hasan Atalay.

Chivas Sandage is the author of *Hidden Drive* (Antrim House, 2012), a finalist for the 2012 ForeWord Book of the Year Awards in poetry and nominated for a Pushcart Prize. Naomi Shihab Nye chose her poem, "Chopping Onions," as runner-up for the *Southern Humanities Review* 2017 Auburn Witness Poetry Prize. Two of her poems received national awards in the 2014 Provincetown Outermost Poetry Contest judged by Marge Piercy. Her essays and poems have appeared widely in magazines, journals, and anthologies. Connecticut Center for the Book at the Connecticut Humanities Council awarded a planning grant for a high school writing program she designed. The Northampton Arts Council, supported in part by the Massachusetts Cultural Council, has awarded artist grants for her writing, teaching, and performance work. She is at work on a narrative nonfiction book about the 2012 double shooting of Kristene Chapa and Mollie Olgin, a young lesbian couple attacked while on a date in Portland, Texas. Chivas is a writing coach and teaches writing workshops and retreats in Connecticut and Massachusetts. Born in Little Rock, Arkansas, she grew up primarily in Houston, Texas. She has also lived in Galveston, Texas; Santa Fe, New Mexico; Northampton, Massachusetts; and New York City. Currently, she lives with her wife in Easthampton, Massachusetts and San Marcos, Texas.

Cory Sisterhenm is a poet and visual artist from Connecticut. She currently works in the Department of English at Sacred Heart University, where she is also a graduate student in Applied Psychology.

Connecticut State University Distinguished Professor, Vivian Shipley teaches at Southern Connecticut State University. In 2015, she published two books, *The Poet* (LaLit Press at Southeastern Louisiana University) and *Perennial* (Negative Capability Press, Mobile, Alabama) which was nominated for the Pulitzer Prize and named the 2016 Paterson Poetry Prize Finalist.

Jamie Stern's poetry collection *Chasing Steam* was published in January 2013. Her poems have appeared in a number of journals and anthologies, among them *Pushing the Envelope: Epistolary Poems* from Lamar University Press, and *The Traveler's Vade Mecum* from Red Hen Press. An attorney in New York City, Jamie is the co-publisher of seven poetry anthologies in honor of Marie Ponsot, *Still Against War* I-VII. She is a member of the board of Poets House, a literary center and poetry library in lower Manhattan.

Wally Swist is a writer and an editor who has recently finished a new book, *Singing for Nothing: Selected Nonfiction as Literary Memoir*, published by The Operating System, in Brooklyn, New York, in 2018. He has published over two hundred essays, articles, and reviews in periodicals such as *The American Book Review, Connecticut River Review, Grolier's Masterplots, The New Haven Advocate*, and *Small Press Review*. His critical essay, a literary biographical monograph, *The Friendship of Two New England Poets: Robert Frost and Robert Francis*, was published by The Edwin Mellen Press. His books of poetry include *Huang Po and the Dimensions of Love* (Southern Illinois University Press, 2012), and he is a co-author of *The Daodejing: An Interpretation*, with David Breeden and Steven Schroeder (Lamar

University Press, 2015). His poems have appeared in such national magazines as *Commonweal, North American Review, Rolling Stone*, and *Yankee*, and Garrison Keillor has read his work on the national radio program The Writers Almanac. He is also a children's book author, infusing a children's classic with poetic prose, the result of which is the new version of Moscow Ballet's *Great Russian Nutcracker* (Talmi Entertainment, 2012).

Larry D. Thomas's poems ("Bluing," "Alzheimer's" and "Primary Colors") were used as the text for a three-part song cycle for mezzo-soprano, saxophone, and piano. The composition, titled "Blue Diminuendo," was composed by Dr. Lon Chaffin, composer-in-residence and Music Department chair of New Mexico State University, and was world-premiered at the Hemmle Recital Hall of Texas Tech University on Sept. 24, 2017. The three performers were mezzo-soprano Sarah Daughtrey, associate professor of music at New Mexico State University; saxophonist David Box of Lubbock; and pianist Justin Badgerow, collaborative pianist for Elizabethtown College in Elizabethtown, Pennsylvania. Additionally, his poem "Dayroom" was selected as first runner-up for the 2017-2018 Switchgrass Review Prize sponsored by Texas A&M University/ Corpus Christi and the Coastal Bend Wellness Foundation of Corpus Christi, Texas.

J. C. Todd was awarded the 2016 Rita Dove Poetry Prize and holds fellowships from the Pew Foundation, the Pennsylvania Council on the Arts, the Ucross, Ragdale and Leeway Foundations, and the international artist exchange program at the Virginia Center for the Creative Arts. Her poetry collections include *FUBAR*, an artist-book collaboration (Lucia Press, 2016), *What Space This Body* (Wind Publications, 2008) and two chapbooks, with poems in the American *Poetry Review, Paris Review, Ekphrasis, THRUSH*, and *Valparaiso Review*. She has taught poetry at Bryn Mawr College and is on the MFA faculty at Rosemont. In 2016, she was a writer-in-residence at Humboldt University in Berlin.

Loretta Diane Walker, a multiple Pushcart Nominee and Best of the Net Nominee, won the 2016 Phyllis Wheatley Book Award for poetry, for her collection *In This House* (Bluelight Press). She was named "Statesman in the Arts" by the Heritage Council of Odessa. In December 2016 she had the rare opportunity to be the commencement speaker for the University of Texas at the Permian Basin. Loretta was honored to be the featured poet in February 2017 for *Red River Review*. Her work has appeared in various literary journals and anthologies, including *River of Earth and Sky*, *Her Texas*, and *Concho River Review*. She has published four collections of poetry. Her most recent collection is *Desert Light*, Lamar University Press. Her manuscript *Word Ghetto* won the 2011 Bluelight Press Book Award.

Sarah Webb is the former poetry and fiction editor of *Crosstimbers*, a multicultural, interdisciplinary journal from the University of Science and Arts of Oklahoma. Her collection *Red Riding Hood's Sister* is published by Virtual Artists Collective (2018). Her collection *Black* (Virtual Artists Collective, 2013) was a finalist for the Oklahoma Book Award and for the Writers' League of Texas Book Award. She is co-leader of an ongoing writing group for Zen and Writing.

Clarence Wolfshohl has been active in the small press as writer and publisher for nearly fifty years. He has published poetry and non-fiction in many journals, both print and online, most recently the e-chapbook *Scattering Ashes* (Virtual Artists Collective, 2016) and the print chapbook *Holy Toledo* (El Grito del Lobo Press, 2017). He lives in the suburbs of Toledo, Missouri, with his dog and cat.

Geraldine Zetzel lives in Lexington, Massachusetts. Currently she leads courses in literature at the Tufts Osher Institute for Lifelong Learning. Her most recent collection, *Traveling Light*, came out in 2016. She is also the author of the full-length *Mapping the Sands* and two chapbooks, *Near Enough to Hear the Words* and *With Both Hands*.